POLICING AND THE COMMUNITY

POLICING AND THE COMMUNITY

Edited by Peter Willmott

Policy Studies Institute

PSI Discussion Paper No. 16

PSI Publications are obtainablefrom all good bookshops, or by visiting the
Institute at 100 Park Village East, London NW1 3SR (01-387 2171)

Sales Representation: Frances Pinter (Publishers) Ltd.
            Orders to: Marston Book Services,
                       P.O. Box 87,
                       Oxford 0X4 1LB

ISBN 0-85374-368-1

Published by Policy Studies Institute
100 Park Village East, London NW1 3SR
Printed by Bourne Offset Ltd.

CONTENTS

CONTENTS

CONTRIBUTORS

Mollie Weatheritt is Deputy Director of the Police Foundation

Joanna Shapland and Jon Vagg are at the Centre for Criminological Research, University of Oxford

Rod Morgan is at the School of Humanities and Social Sciences, University of Bath

Jon Bright is Co-ordinator of the Safe Neighbourhoods Unit

David Smith and Peter Willmott are Senior Fellows at the Policy Studies Institute

1 INTRODUCTION
Peter Willmott

These papers were originally given at a seminar at the Policy Studies Institute in October 1986. The development of community policing is part of a more general trend to introduce notions of community into policy and practice, and the seminar, chaired by Robin Guthrie, Director of the Joseph Rowntree Memorial Trust, was part of a broader Rowntree-supported review of that trend.

The review is looking at a range of community-labelled policies and initiatives, from community care to community radio, from community architecture to community education. These applications vary in what they are trying to do, but some general themes can be identified: a reaction against the scale and remoteness of many of the institutions of contemporary society; a belief that people themselves can - and wish to - contribute to the solution of their problems; and a search for policies and practices which strengthen and co-operate with the voluntary and informal sectors rather than working against them.

The main aim of the review is to help clear away some of the ambiguities about community initiatives and policies, seeking to identify objectives and to see how far these are being achieved. One interest is to explore how far there are similarities and differences between the various applications - on the familiar argument that, like all comparative study, this can encourage clearer thought and a more rigorous examination of particular cases. Examples of common issues are the problem of representativeness (how far do those who claim to represent the community really do so?) and the difficulties of meshing together public services (whether, for example, policing or social welfare) with what people do informally.

The seminar was not just about community policing as it is usually conceived by the Home Office and the police service but about a wider range of issues, including in particular the contribution made by the 'informal policing' that people do for themselves. The discussion covered not only such operational measures as increasing the number of foot patrols, encouraging crime prevention, instituting inter-agency collaboration and participating in consultative committees, but also police cooperation with local people in dealing with problems (the paper by Joanna Shapland and Jon Vagg), the contribution of local authorities and other bodies in preventing crime (Jon

Bright's paper) and police accountability to the community, including for example the lay visitors to police stations scheme. The aim was to arrive at some assessment of where community policing, in this broad sense, had got to and in particular how it related to the 'informal social control' exercised by people themselves.

A seductive word

The term community is used loosely and in many senses, all deriving from the original basis of the word, which of course refers to people who have something in common. A useful distinction can be made between the *territorial community*, defined by geography and meaning the people who live in a particular area; the *interest community*, a set of people with something in common other than just territory (the black community, the Jewish community, the gay community); and the *attachment community*, where there is the kind of attachment to people or place which gives rise to a 'sense of community'.

These three types can overlap. First, though interest communities are often geographically dispersed, many are local - for example, a local territorial community might contain, among others, several communities of church and chapel-goers, a community of business people and a community of Asian residents. Secondly, attachment and community sense can bind people together in territorial communities or interest communities.

Separating out these various meanings may have the advantage of drawing attention to the fact that the people living in a particular area do not always feel a sense of attachment to each other or to the place, nor necessarily share the same priorities as their neighbours; indeed in complex modern societies they seldom do either to any substantial extent. The distinction may also put us on our guard against the warm, almost mystical, feelings that can be stirred by the word community. One of its dangers, as David Smith points out, is that it 'encourages skilful jumps' from one meaning to another. It can conceal more than it reveals, and is often intended to. Those advocating a new initiative, and similarly those attacking or defending a particular point of view, often invoke the community in support of their case, without making it clear which community they mean or in what sense it is likely to be affected.

The research evidence

The seminar set out to bring together as a basis for discussion on the one hand some research findings and on the other the experience of some practitioners. The researchers, looking in turn at different attempts to turn the notion of community policing into reality, presented their accounts of the record so far. The picture that emerges from their papers is a fairly consistent one.

Mollie Weatheritt reviews the experience of community policing to date in terms of two important initiatives - more foot patrol and the encouragement of community-based crime prevention. She spells out the problems that these initiatives are trying to tackle and then presents the evidence about how effective they are. In line with her earlier book (Weatheritt, 1986), she suggests that there is little or no sign that they have yet made any measurable difference; indeed she concludes that 'Whilst community policing ideas have been useful in stimulating debate and action, answers to policing problems cannot be found in community policing philosophy nor in the practice to which it has given rise'.

The research by Joanna Shapland and Jon Vagg was unique in looking at the informal policing carried out by residents and local business people, and at the relationship between that and policing by the police. They show that the police view of their task is usually different from that of local people, that in any event police officers themselves vary in their perspectives depending on their position within the force, and that in general the characteristic police response does not blend at all easily with what people do by way of policing. The balance is a delicate one, and formal policing can, in their words, 'easily undermine informal policing by the public'.

Rod Morgan's description of the composition and characteristic development of consultative committees and his analysis of their work suggest that, although they can be of value in ventilating local problems and promoting practical cooperative solutions, they have not had much success in building, in any serious way, the hoped-for partnership between the police and the community. Morgan suggests various explanations for this failure: 'confusion and ignorance' on the part of committee members, the lack of education to help them in their role, the negative response to the police and the committees - for understandable reasons - from certain elements in the community, and the reluctance of police forces - for equally understandable reasons - to provide adequate information to the committees or to treat them as much more than a public relations forum.

Jon Bright's main argument is that crime prevention should be led by local authorities rather than the police, should be supported by investment in infrastructure and social facilities as an alternative to more spending on the criminal justice system, and should draw heavily on local people's views about priorities and ideas for action. But in the process of arguing that case he concludes on the basis of the experience of the Safe Neighbourhoods Unit in London council estates that, although the police have an important role to play, home beats are generally too large, police contacts with the local community limited and 'unproductive' and relationships with blacks do not seem to have been improved by neighbourhood policing.

David Smith, in his broader review of research to date, confirms that the accumulating evidence is that in practice the application of community policing ideas 'has made little difference or has not produced the intended results'. He suggests that there are fundamental problems in trying to develop better relationships between the police and the community - problems that the enthusiasts for community policing have not yet faced.

The picture that emerges from the research is thus on the whole a disappointing one. A cynic might draw the conclusion that the new initiatives are more an exercise in rhetoric, in public relations, than in building a new partnership between the police and the community.

Striking a balance
That is of course only one interpretation. On the other side, some of the police officers attending the seminar, and some other participants, cited what they saw

as more encouraging examples from their own experience.

Can these apparently contradictory perspectives be reconciled? One starting point in trying to reconcile them is that the research papers are by no means wholly negative in their conclusions. If for the most part they fail to present conclusive evidence of success, most of them also acknowledge there have been some successes, albeit modest. Furthermore, most have positive suggestions to offer about how performance might be improved.

It has to be said too that community policing is relatively new, and that it has not so far been the subject of much research. If there is little evidence to warrant enthusiasm, it is nevertheless arguably too early to make comprehensive judgements on the basis of fairly limited innovations, evaluated over a relatively short period of time. As one police officer put it at the seminar, early successes should hardly be expected, since the police service is engaged on a long-term investment in the minds of its young officers.

In any event, nobody would argue that the objectives of community policing are either unworthy or *completely* impossible of achievement. The spirit is right, one might say, even if the implementation is proving much more difficult than expected. As most people would agree, there is no real alternative to a community-based approach to policing, difficult though it may be to give substance to the idea. What has to be done is to ensure that the efforts to introduce and develop it are sensibly directed, drawing as far as possible on the research to date.

The dilemmas
It is clear that the problems of implementation are not all detailed technical ones. Some of them are fundamental and turn on the inevitable tensions and conflicts in the role of the police in a democratic society. These are touched on in several papers, and are discussed explicitly by Rod Morgan and David Smith. They both refer to three crucial dilemmas. First, most of the functions of the police are, in David Smith's word, 'adversarial' and therefore can only with difficulty be reconciled with the creation of consensus. Secondly, the establishment of goodwill is difficult because in any locality the police have to deal not with one community but with several and almost inevitably impinge on those communities in different ways. Thirdly, there can be basic conflicts between the rule of law and two key features of community policing - decentralisation and 'flexibility' of treatment.

These very problems may well help to explain the attraction to many senior police officers, civil servants and politicians of a 'community policing' ideology. As most of the seminar papers recognise, the police today are under immense pressure - much greater than in the past. They are caught in a series of conflicting demands. For example, all opinion surveys show that the overwhelming majority of people want more policemen on the beat; but they also want a rapid response when they dial 999 (see, for example, Jones, Maclean and Young, 1986). The police are expected somehow to reconcile differences within the community and differences between themselves and some community elements whose members may be hostile. In a climate of growing sensitivity to minority interests and ever-present fear that confrontation could lead to violence, the police are expected both to keep the peace and to avoid provocation. It is understandable that the notion of community policing might seem to offer some solution, if only in presentational terms, to these almost irreconcilable tensions.

It is, however, much more difficult than it might at first seem to introduce community policing as a serious exercise, and there is little value to the police or the community (in its various meanings) of a mere PR exercise or a 'bolt-on' extra, to use the terms employed by Paul Ekblom in an earlier paper exploring the same dilemmas (Ekblom, 1986). The seminar papers, together with the discussion they inspired, show in clear terms the main dilemmas that need to be resolved, and they also suggest some of the ways to resolve them.

One conclusion concerns the issue of local consensus and conflict already touched on. The days of community consensus have passed, if they ever existed. Some sections of the local population have different interests from others, and different relationships with the police, as is shown by the Broadwater Farm inquiry (Gifford Report, 1986). Neighbourhoods differ in population mix, in homogeneity and heterogeneity, and therefore in the extent to which there are such conflicts and to which they pose problems. It is essential to recognise openly that the conflicts exist.

Nevertheless, there is some common ground in all districts, as the Islington crime survey indicates (Jones, Maclean and Young, 1986). People in Islington differ in the priorities they give to different problems, and in what they think should be done about them, but not in the basic need for order and safety, or in particular for the police to respond promptly to crime and to deter it effectively. So a first task for police forces - and this is something on which local surveys can help - is to identify such unanimity as does exist and seek ways of building on it.

That is not the end of the matter. It has to be recognised that there are sometimes deep-seated conflicts of interest between different sets of people in a locality, and important differences in their respective relationships with the police. So there needs to be some machinery which can make it possible for *negotiation* to take place where necessary between the different interests and the police.

Another problem is that of scale. Unless they operate locally, formal structures for collaboration with the community are unlikely to connect with local concerns. Earlier research has shown that people's own notions of their local community or neighbourhood embrace a very small geographical area (Willmott, 1986), and the point is confirmed by the Shapland and Vagg study. As Rod Morgan points out, in terms of such localised interests, consultative committees serving a population of 100,000 or so 'operate in the stratosphere'. There is a strong case for creating, and insofar as they already exist encouraging, police/public forums at a smaller geographical scale.

As well as consultative procedures at the local level, more thought needs to be given to the arrangements through which representatives of the community can influence policing policy and practice at the force level. This issue is raised in the papers by Rod Morgan and Jon Bright. If, as I have just suggested, there is a need for a formal structure within which an accommodation can be negotiated between the police and particular local interests, that strengthens the case for a structure within which the police are answerable to an effective body representing the wider public or community interest. This almost certainly means something different from the existing police authorities. The next government, whatever its political complexion, will presumably have to come to some decision if only about Greater London where, unlike everywhere else, there is at present no police authority other than the Home Secretary. The opportunity should be taken to consider change over a wider geographical canvas. A range of alternatives to the present arrangements need to be reviewed, as part of a careful and cool-headed examination.

Whatever the future arrangements at the force level, they are unlikely to work effectively unless the authorities representing the public have enough staff of their own, enough resources to collect information for themselves about police performance, and appropriate training for their members in how to do their job. There is a direct parallel here with what Rod Morgan says about the current weaknesses of local consultative committees, and the remedies for them. At both levels a genuine partnership between the police and the community they serve depends on official recognition, backed by resources, of the need to educate and support the community's representatives.

The Home Office and the police forces will need to face up to the challenges posed in this collection of papers. The police, in collaboration with researchers, will need to be more explicit about the objectives of specific practices - what exactly is the problem that a particular community policing initiative is intended to solve, what is the precise case for the proposed solution? They will also need to be clear about the appropriate criteria of achievement - in other words, about how to measure success or failure when innovations are introduced. Further independent research, better monitoring and more careful analysis of objectives and of what is happening on the ground can help those inside and outside the police service to develop a better understanding of the issues and give clearer indications of what is needed for the future.

References

Ekblom, P. (1986) 'Community policing: obstacles and issues', in P. Willmott, (editor) *The Debate About Community: papers from a seminar on Community in Social Policy*, Discussion Paper 13, London, Policy Studies Institute.
Gifford Report (1986) *The Broadwater Farm Inquiry: report of the independent inquiry into disturbances of October 1985 at the Broadwater Farm Estate, Tottenham*, London, The Inquiry.
Jones, T., Maclean, B. and Young, J. (1986) *The Islington Crime Survey: crime, victimisation and policing in inner-city London*, Aldershot, Gower.
Weatheritt, M. (1986) *Innovations in Policing*, London, Croom Helm.
Willmott, P. (1986) *Social Networks, Informal Care and Public Policy*, Research Report 655, London, Policy Studies Institute.

2 COMMUNITY POLICING NOW

Mollie Weatheritt

It has become part of conventional wisdom to see community policing as providing a coherent set of answers to policing problems whose solutions have so far eluded us. The prescriptions that community policing offers tend to be seen as self-evidently desirable, appropriate and sensible; and the state of affairs to which community policing is put forward as a response is usually taken for granted as being in need of reform. In this paper I shall treat neither community policing solutions nor the problems which these sometimes set out to tackle as self-evident. My aim is to try to assess empirically some of the assumptions that proponents of community policing make about what the problems are; to take stock of what is known about community policing practice and effectiveness; and to raise some questions about the failure of community policing ideas to tackle fundamental issues about the police role or to provide a framework for considering those issues.

Community policing is a conveniently elastic term which is often loosely used to accommodate virtually any policing activity of which its proponents approve. There is no agreed definition of what community policing is or ought to be or could be. At one level the term has become little more than a consensual rallying cry, used to convey a sense of nostalgia and of exhortation. It summons up a world we have lost, a golden age of consensual policing which is contrasted, implicitly or explicitly, with an undesirable present and which stands as inspiration for a better future. At another level, community policing is used as a convenient shorthand for what its advocates wish to see become the dominant ethos of policing: an ethos which emphasises notions of service, the sensitive use of discretion, conciliation, consultation and negotiation. Here the contrast is with a policing rhetoric and style which are characterised as having lost touch with what the public wants, threatening of civil liberties, invasive, oppressive, alienating and ineffective. At another and more detailed level community policing is used to describe a set of specific initiatives or practices, the best known of which are attempts to return more bobbies to the beat. In an earlier contribution in the PSI series, Paul Ekblom (1986) listed as features of community policing practice: community constables; specialist community liaison officers; crimes analysis; police discos and clubs for young people; schools liaison; police shops; community surveys; inter-agency approaches such as victim support, juvenile bureaux, joint casework and joint training; and local consultative committees. To this list one might perhaps add specialist panels; neighbourhood watch; physical security improvement programmes instigated by the police; and crime prevention liaison arrangements. In keeping with the disparate nature of these proposals, many contrasts are implied here. Overall, the emphasis is on pragmatic, small-scale and locally-based interventions rather than on the working out of a grand design which is expected fundamentally to alter the nature of the police as an institution.

Community policing may be presented as a more or less coherent set of ideas, ideals and practices, as is done by John Alderson, the most notable exponent of community policing (Alderson, 1979). Or the connection between the various elements which are said to comprise the community policing approach may be left vague and tenuous or even be coincidental. Nonetheless, community policing activities, disparate though they may be, have important features in common. Broadly speaking, community policing is about emphasising and encouraging the development of preventive and non-conflictual aspects of policing and giving them more status than they currently have within the police and more impact outside it. By these means it is hoped and expected that policing will be made more effective - both directly through the capacity of community policing methods to prevent and detect crime, and indirectly by conferring legitimacy on policing as an activity and the police as an institution. The means by which these aims are to be achieved are the cultivation of improved relationships with the public, or certain sections of it, in order to improve the amount and quantity of information the police receive, and to impress on people the responsibility for policing that they themselves should take.

In the rest of this paper I concentrate on two main aspects of community policing practice: patrol, and (more briefly) measures to involve institutions and individuals other than the police in crime prevention. I leave aside the politics of community policing - the structures and forms of dialogue through which the community expresses its interests and concerns and tries to influence policing policy. Although no comprehensive overview of community policing can properly leave out issues of accountability, these are dealt with by other contributors. My concern here is with arguments for changes in the substance of operational policing and what these changes are expected to achieve, rather than with the formal mechanisms which exist or ought to exist for articulating and giving political force to those arguments.

Patrol: the problems
The community policing arguments about patrol go as follows.

The introduction of policing technologies in the late 1960s and early 1970s, particularly cars and personal radios, has fundamentally altered policing methods and policing styles and has thereby upset some supposed previously harmonious state of relations between police and public. Cars are seen to have created a physical barrier between police and public so that opportunities for informal and non-adversarial interaction - from the ritual 'good morning' to more extended opportunities to give information or seek advice from an accessible foot patrol officer - are greatly reduced. As well as reducing the opportunities for this kind of interaction, policing technology is also seen to have encouraged the growth of a more distant, less conciliatory and more abrasive policing style. A weak version of this argument, often put forward by senior police officers, is that officers who patrol in cars 'don't know how to talk to people'. A stronger version stresses the psychological effects of long periods of uneventfulness and boredom spent waiting for something to happen, interspersed with the tension and excitement generated by responding to emergency calls. In the words of two non-police advocates of community policing, this 'abrupt variation of work can give rise to situations where frustration and irritation surface naturally'. The result is inept, officious or abrasive handling of incidents (Baldwin and Kinsey, 1982, p.44).

Another version of the argument stresses the dangers of technological over-kill. The ability of officers to call for help over the radio system and the knowledge that help will arrive quickly mean that officers have less incentive to develop a conciliatory approach towards dangerous or potentially dangerous incidents, and are more likely to act coercively in situations where a conciliatory and persuasive approach would be more appropriate. The effect of this change in policing styles has been characterised not only as an instrumental one to do with the way officers approach particular tasks, but also as a moral one. John Alderson contrasts police officers working together with the officer who works alone in a way which unequivocally favours the latter: 'Where officers operate as one-man forces they are inclined to develop superior policing characteristics', which include fairness, resolve, overall caring instinct, integrity, kindness, courage and respect for human dignity (Alderson, 1979, Chapter 3). On this argument, reliance on policing technologies has changed not only the way in which policing is done, but also the values to which the police as an institution seek to give expression.

Advocates of community policing have tended to characterise the kinds of changes I have described in a largely negative way. The terms used to describe them - response, reactive or fire-brigade policing - invariably carry pejorative connotations. Baldwin and Kinsey, for example, in a book advocating wide-scale policing reforms, many of which are borrowed from Alderson's vision of a community policing future, regard reactive policing as entirely synonymous with the 'drift away from policing by consent'. It is 'the developed form of non-consensual policing' (Baldwin and Kinsey, 1982, pp.217-8). Alderson's own view of reactive policing is a more temperate one, but he thinks that there are dangers nonetheless if the police fail to strike the right balance between reactive work and its claimed obverse: proactive or preventive policing. 'Too much reliance on reactive policing can only lead to estrangement between the police and the public ... Estrangement can lead to public indifference, to misunderstanding, to suspicion, to animosity and even ... to hatred' (Alderson, op.cit., p.236).

The argument goes wider than the way in which reactive policing is claimed to affect the public's view of the police. If public cooperation is forfeited, the jobs of detecting and preventing crime become more difficult. If people mistrust the police, they will be less likely to give them information about crime. Police thus get to hear of less crime and are given less information relevant to clearing up the crime which does come to their notice. Detection rates fall, relationships deteriorate further, people entrust the police with even less information than before and so the spiral of decreasing effectiveness and worsening police/public relationships continues.

A related set of arguments has to do with the effects of firebrigading on the ability of the police to prevent crime. Here firebrigading is cast in a more popular role and the police as victims not of its failings but of its success. The argument is that, in advertising their availability and willingness to respond when called and in seeking to ensure that their response is quick and efficient, the police have created an increased demand for their services. As demand has increased, so the police have responded by committing more resources to meeting it; this has been done at the expense of resources committed to preventive work. As preventive policing has decreased, so crime has risen. More crime has given rise to more demand for response policing and so on. Thus another spiral of decreasing effectiveness is set in train. Another strand of this argument is to do with the effects of reactive policing, not on the time available to do other types of work, but on collective organisational psychology. Reactive patrol officers, it is said, are rarely in a position to see their work as anything more than a series of seemingly disconnected incidents, while the reactive response is essentially a form of crisis management concerned mainly with the immediate and short-term. These features of their work discourage officers from seeing problems in the round and hence from undertaking the kind of thinking that is required to plan and implement long-term preventive strategies.

Patrol: the solutions

The community policing solutions involving patrol seek to put these assumed trends or states of affairs into reverse or to compensate for them or mitigate them in some way. In essence they involve attempts to divert public attention and police resources away from the kind of work done by officers in cars (there is a tendency for reactive policing to be regarded as virtually irrelevant in the community policing scheme of things) and towards foot-beat officers, particularly community constables. The arguments for doing this may be spelt out in a fairly detailed way, or they may leave unspoken or take for granted a host of assumptions about the nature of police work and what it can achieve.

Moves to return more officers to foot patrol are usually justified on the ground that this is what the public wants. From here it is but a short step to assuming that meeting this preference will automatically deliver the kinds of policing goods that the public values. The arguments in favour of having more foot patrol officers are in essence the converse of those deployed against reactive policing. Officers on foot are seen to be more approachable than officers in cars and the more of them there are, the more will opportunities increase for friendly non-adversarial contact between police and public. Increased contact will make for better relationships with the public, who will then be more ready to give the police information about crime and criminals. This argument is applied with more force to community constables who, because of their continuing attachment to a small area and their brief to get to know the people who live and work there, are able to accumulate a detailed knowledge of what goes on. This knowledge helps the police detect more crime. Familiarity with a small area means that the officer responsible for it can gain a broad picture of what is going on and this knowledge provides a basis for planning work around preventive strategies. Finally, their privileged access and knowledge mean that community officers are able to invoke informal methods of social control without recourse to more formal mechanisms of law enforcement. The result is a less abrasive, more consensual and more conciliatory policing style which contributes to a positive image of policing and is more effective in achieving the traditional aims of prevention and detection of crime.

Patrol: the evidence
Can the assumptions which the advocates of community policing make about its superior image and effectiveness be sustained? The evidence is patchy and equivocal, but it suggests that the foundations on which the community policing edifice has been erected are not always sound and that the claims made for its superior effectiveness have been exaggerated.

People want more foot patrol. Anecdotal evidence unequivocally supports this. Evidence from surveys is also strong. For example in the Merseyside Crime Survey, eight out of 10 people said they wanted more officers to patrol on foot (Kinsey, 1984). The PSI survey of Londoners found that seven out of 10 people wanted this (Smith, 1983, Chapter 7). In a Police Foundation survey of one inner London ward (in Notting Hill), nearly everyone who was interviewed said either that they thought it was fairly important (20 per cent) or very important (77 per cent) that police officers should patrol on foot (Hibberd, 1985, Table 6.20). In a survey carried out by Northamptonshire Police, when people were asked 'What particular job would you like to see police officers doing in the district?', 'More foot patrols' was by far the most popular response. Sixty per cent of people wanted the police to patrol more and five out of six of these said they wanted the police to do so on foot (Moss and Bucknall, 1983, Table 37).

Reactive policing is unpopular. It has worsened police/public relations. Foot patrol is popular, but is its converse - police patrolling in cars - unpopular? The evidence is more mixed. In the PSI survey, 70 per cent of people thought that too many police patrolled in cars and only 20 per cent wanted more car patrols. In the Northamptonshire survey, nobody spontaneously mentioned that they wanted the police to patrol in cars. But in the Police Foundation survey, nearly three-quarters of people said that they thought it was either fairly important (42 per cent) or very important (32 per cent) that the police should patrol in cars.

These apparent differences are probably largely accounted for by the ways in which survey questions have been formulated; for example, whether people have been asked open-ended questions about what they think the police should do, or whether they have been asked to rank or endorse a set of hypothetical priorities. Another difficulty in interpreting survey results is that survey questions about car and foot patrol tend to be framed in general and abstract terms. People have not been asked *why* they want more foot patrol, or *why* they think car patrol is important. Often it is difficult or impossible to infer from their expressed preferences for certain kinds of patrol deployment what kinds of policing services people think they will be getting as a result. In several surveys people have been asked to rank or assess what objectives they think the police should pursue, for example whether the police should investigate crime or catch criminals and, if so, what kinds of crime and criminals should attract priority, or whether the police should control traffic. But these objectives can rarely be linked in a simple or straightforward way to the kinds of views people express about how the police should be deployed.

An important exception to this relates to car patrol. People strongly support one of its main objectives - enabling the police to respond quickly to 999 calls. The Islington and Merseyside crime surveys and the Police Foundation survey of Notting Hill put this at the top of people's policing priorities and in all three surveys fast response was rated as very important by virtually everyone (Jones, Maclean and Young, 1986; Kinsey, 1984; Hibberd, 1985). Contrary to received wisdom, the essence of firebrigading is extremely popular.

Reactive policing is popular not only in the abstract; people also like it when they get it. In a Home Office study of over 300 telephoned calls to the police for help to which a patrol was subsequently despatched, 90 per cent of callers said they were satisfied with the police response. An ever greater number (96 per cent) were satisfied with the way in which the officers had dealt with them on a personal level (Ekblom and Heal, 1982, pp.51-3). In those rare cases where the caller expressed dissatisfaction with the police response, the officers' personal manner was not at issue. People's main concerns were that the police had not responded quickly enough or, when they arrived, had refused to take responsibility for dealing with the caller's problem.

This Home Office study suggests that car patrol officers only rarely failed to act calmly, sympathetically and authoritatively (ibid, p.56). Although it was small and limited to one force, the study undermines the claim that car patrol officers lack competence in dealing with the public; that they routinely act aggressively or in a non-conciliatory way; or that having officers patrol in cars is bad for police/public relations. Of course officers' ability to handle incidents and encounters of various kinds varies a great deal (Smith and Gray, 1983, Chapter 3; Southgate and Ekblom, 1986). But it seems more likely that policing styles and approaches vary *within* different types of patrol than that the method of transport officers use is a major influence on how they behave.

Reactive policing has led to falling detection rates. Although the clear-up rate has fallen since the late 1960s, the trend has not been a consistent one. In the years immediately following police investment in cars and personal radios, when it seems reasonable to assume that increased numbers of officers began to patrol in cars, the clear-up rate actually rose: from 40 per cent in 1966 to 47 per cent in 1973. Taken in isolation, these figures do not support the contention that reactive policing has led to falling detection rates. On the contrary, they undermine it. In the 12 years since 1973 the clear-up rate has fallen consistently each year. In 1974 it stood at 44 per cent; by 1985 it was 35 per cent. There are, however, no comparable historical data available on patrol deployment over this period. The clear-up rate is in any case a very rough and ready measure of what causes concern, which is people's supposed increasing unwillingness to pass on to the police the information that the latter need to detect crime. The argument about whether or not this has happened can be little more than speculation.

Reactive policing has been at the expense of preventive policing. The argument is that the police service has become obsessed with reaction and has put less effort than it should have done into preventive activities. As before, there are no historical data on how the balance of patrol deployment (car; foot; community constable) has changed over time. Nor are there historical data on the kinds of activities undertaken by these different officers. It is also less easy than it looks to classify particular policing activities as either reactive or preventive. Many patrol activities combine, or could combine, aspects of both. Thus response policing carries with it many opportunities for prevention, for example the officer responding to a burglary is able to offer advice on home security in circumstances where that advice will hit home hardest. Conversely, his so-called preventive patrol colleague, working on foot and to a greater extent freed from the demands of reaction, may find it more difficult to do preventive work; fewer opportunities are presented to him; indeed he is expected to create his own. (There is some evidence that community constables do indeed find preventive work difficult: see below.) It is not that reactive policing takes up time that would otherwise be used to do planned, preventive work, it is that planned preventive work is inherently more difficult to do.

The argument that more reaction has meant less time for prevention is also undermined by the fact that over the last 20 years - over the period in which reactive policing is seen to have increased - the police have created more specialisms specifically to do prevention. Prevention has come to be seen not just as something which gets fitted around traditional patrol activity, but as something which is planned and carried out separately and for which designated officers (crime prevention officers or community liaison officers) are given a distinct responsibility. Whether these developments have been effective is of course another matter, but they cast doubt on the assumption that reactive policing *per se* has resulted in the police attending less and less to the preventive aspects of their work.

I have argued so far that many of the assumptions that are made about the undesirability and ill effects of reactive policing are either not supported by evidence or run counter to it. If the problems have been misrepresented, what of the solutions? How have they been devised and implemented and what evidence is there of their effectiveness?

One of the difficulties in answering this question is lack of information. Attempts to return more officers to the beat, whether to general foot patrol or as community constables, have tended to be implemented as though they raised few or no significant questions about what tasks these officers should be carrying out. There is a sense in which the community policing solution remains a black box. One of the reasons for this is that the community policing arguments have sounded so self-evidently sensible and so seductive that the solutions have been pursued more at a symbolic level than at a practical level. We have been asked to take them on trust and have been willing to do so. In practice, there are a number of contradictions in what is sometimes expected from community-based officers. Community policing concepts have glossed over these contradictions.

The supposed superiority of foot patrol. It is now widely argued, mainly on the basis of patrol studies carried out in America, that officers patrolling on foot are no more or less likely to prevent crime than officers who patrol in cars (Clarke and Hough, 1984). There is no comparable published research for England and Wales. What we have instead is a number of studies, many of them carried out by the police themselves, which have set out to assess small-scale, local or experimental schemes, most of which have involved deploying community constables or increasing their numbers.

Most of these studies purport to show that such schemes are desirable, that they are welcomed by local residents, that they improve the visibility of police, encourage friendly interaction between police and public, reduce crime and improve detection rates. Insofar as the work of community beat officers is described in these studies, it is given an appearance of constructiveness and purposefulness. The treatment of community officers by the rest of the force strikes the only negative note in these accounts: their work is portrayed as inadequately rewarded and poorly integrated with that of other officers. However, these difficulties are more than compensated for by community officers' unqualified success in dealing with their public.

I have argued elsewhere that the evidence on which the conclusion of these studies is based is patchy, partial or ambiguous and that the incidence of policing successes which they purport to demonstrate is inversely related to the rigour with which schemes have been evaluated (Weatheritt, 1983 and 1986). But this conclusion should not be used to dismiss the efficacy of changes in patrol based on community policing rationales. This is because in many schemes there has been a failure to provide community-based officers with a set of tasks that are rationally related to a clear conception of their role. One effect of this is the kind of situation described in a Home Office study which looked at the kinds of activities undertaken by 300 community officers in five forces (Brown and Iles, 1985). The presumed core of their work, 'community involvement', took up only 14 per cent of these officers' time. Over half of that time was spent withdrawn from their beat, doing other policing tasks.

Patrol: some issues
The role that community policing would assign to officers currently has insufficient practical outcomes. It is a conceptual not a practical role. If we try to define those practical outcomes and the work that is needed to achieve them, some interesting paradoxes emerge. The community policing 'solution' becomes neither a coherent nor an obvious one, nor does it necessarily contrast markedly with the kind of policing that is said to constitute the problem. There is a sense in which community policing is and can only be 'more of the same'.

Although they are nowhere fully spelt out by the advocates of community policing, ideas about what community officers should do include the following: patrol; community involvement; planned preventive work to tackle recurrent problems in the area for which an officer is responsible; and the acquisition of knowledge relevant to the purposes of policing, particularly crime detection.

Patrol. There is in effect no community policing theory of patrol other than that it ought to be done. As a way of providing a job for constables, this seems less than adequate. Patrol in itself fulfils at least one function: that of providing a police presence on the streets. But providing more than this requires that constables undertake specific activities which it is possible to specify to them and which serve some purpose with which they can identify.

One of these purposes may be community involvement at a simple and mundane level (the ritual 'good morning') although this is unlikely to provide either a real sense of purpose or adequate job satisfaction. One of the ways of improving both is to draw community officers into what is essentially reactive policing, albeit at a slower pace. It is interesting that police concern with returning more officers to beat work has coincided with attempts to implement systems of graded response which are designed to reduce the need for a fast response to every call for service.

One effect of this development has been to give foot patrol officers and community beat officers more response work (West Midlands Police, 1982; Hampshire Constabulary, 1981). While it seems sensible to use community officers in this way, and it gives them something purposeful to do, such reactive activities sit somewhat uneasily with community policing rhetoric.

Community involvement. The fundamental question here is what is community involvement for? Community involvement is usually recognised as worthwhile in itself and for its ambassadorial and public relations functions. In community policing terms, however, it is supposed to be something more, not just an activity but also a style. If this is to be the case, then that style needs to be harnessed to other policing functions.

Planned problem-solving is an obvious candidate for this. The idea that planned problem-solving should form a major part of community beat work has only recently come to be seen as part of the community policing package and as facilitated by community policing philosophy. The idea is that the beat officers' close knowledge of their areas and their relative freedom from other policing duties allow problems to be identified and likely solutions implemented by bringing in non-police resources. I return to some of the problems in doing this when I examine community crime prevention, and other problems relating to planning are referred to in David Smith's paper. As yet, we have virtually no information about whether or how planned police work is done by beat officers or whether such activity achieves its objectives.

Acquiring beat knowledge or intelligence gathering. The intimate knowledge of their area that beat officers are expected to acquire is by no means expected just to remain with them. Their knowledge is seen as making a vital and even unique contribution to crime detection and to the maintenance of public order. In this respect it is of interest that, of the 15 duties of an area constable defined by a Home Office working party on operational efficiency and management, over half are concerned with the acquisition of information about crime and criminals and the importance of passing this information on to other members of the force (Home Office, 1967, p.142). This implied definition of the beat officers' role is unambiguously concerned with law enforcement. This is somewhat at odds with community policing rhetoric, which tends to play down the police's enforcement role, to overlook it, or to actively disapprove of it. Baldwin and Kinsey, for example, classify intelligence gathering as 'hard' policing and explicitly contrast it with community policing. Yet it is difficult to see what else than what amounts to the acquisition of intelligence should provide the focus of constables' information-gathering activities if their prized local knowledge is to have any practical outcome. Whilst nobody would deny that what information officers collect should be a matter of public concern, community policing ideas have so far proved of little help in defining the legitimate extent of the police role. On the contrary, they have tended to discourage rational discussion of it.

I have argued that, in terms of foot patrol, giving substance to community policing generalities entails in part a more incisive rethinking of policing jobs and in part a return to the kinds of activities which are said to have constituted the problem in the first place. There are also good management reasons for doing this. If, as Baldwin and Kinsey argue, community constables 'are very difficult to control in ways other than firing them with commitment to an idea' (pp.250-1), we are left with nothing of substance from which to judge their achievements. This is tantamount to saying that community police officers are unaccountable - a somewhat ironic position in wiew of the emphasis that community policing advocates usually place on making the police more accountable. Furthermore, if there is to be nothing but idealism to show for community policing, it is destined to remain in that marginal position which its advocates currently bewail.

Community policing and crime prevention
Setting out a distinctively community policing approach to crime prevention is something of an academic exercise. The idea that 'the community' should be an important part of organised crime prevention has formed a central tenet of official thinking for at least 20 years, thus considerably predating the current vogue for community policing. Not only has the idea that the community must play its part in preventing crime been regularly reiterated during this period; it has also been translated into a variety of institutional arrangements and practical initiatives, such as the Home Office Standing Conference on Crime Prevention and local crime prevention panels. A community-based approach to crime prevention is thus neither particularly distinctive nor particularly new. What is at issue is the ways in which 'the community' is defined or identified for different purposes and the terms in which ideas about community are used to support different policies and practices or are expected to determine them.

The main rationale for community crime prevention is the rather obvious one that because the police do not cause crime they can hardly be held solely or even mainly responsible for preventing it. Who is responsible and to what degree is dependent on where the causes of crime are seen to lie, and on the ease and readiness with which the causes can be manipulated to serve officially defined ends. Official policy has three main strands, each dependent on a different notion of cause and of community. The first relates to the idea of the community as everyone, but especially owners of property. The official response here is to try to get people to be more conscious of the risks of crime and more diligent in protecting themselves and their property. Make the public less apathetic and less careless, the argument goes, and crime will be reduced.

The second strand of official policy rests on trying to create a community of interest amongst organisations and institutions which are responsible for the welfare of others or whose actions and policies can create conditions in which crime is more or less likely. The argument is that such organisations have been ignorant, careless or unconcerned about the effects of their actions on crime. Policy is therefore concerned with educating them as to their responsibilities, encouraging them to collect relevant information or providing them with it, and exhorting them to devise coordinated strategies which will make best use of the knowledge, skills and power that each has.

The third strand of official policy is based on the assumption that the growth of crime is associated with the breakdown of community cohesion and informal social control. While the first two strands of official policy are sometimes seen as primarily tackling the symptoms of crime, this strand is more consciously directed at root-causes. The 'community' which this approach usually takes as its starting point is the neighbourhood. The remedial action takes in neighbourhood watch and community development of various kinds.

The police role in community crime prevention
The strands of official policy outlined above imply different roles for the police. Since the establishment of the specialist crime prevention service in the 1960s, the police role has been largely conceived as reaching the public at large. Crime prevention officers have put their main effort into general publicity campaigns and advising individuals on the security of their premises. This conception of the police role is essentially a minimalist and reactive one. This may or may not be appropriate (an issue I return to below). Whatever the case, this traditional approach has been seen as failing to deliver sufficient crime prevention goods (Clarke and Mayhew, 1980; Weatheritt, 1986).

The failure of traditional police crime prevention is one of the reasons why policy-makers have found it appropriate to move the spotlight to other agencies. But while this has been done to boost the effectiveness of crime prevention efforts, defining an appropriate police role has become more problematic and begins to get contentious. Once agencies begin to work together, the police may become privy to information to which they would not previously have had access. Many agencies resist this (see, for example, Blaber, 1979, on the Devon and Cornwall multi-agency experiment). In addition, although it often makes sense for the police to provide helpful and detailed information about crime, it is by no means obvious that they should take the lead in initiating and sustaining cooperation between agencies or defining solutions to crime problems. The police have been criticised for wishing to hijack inter-agency initiatives and for attempting to use community crime prevention for their own ends. Yet the police are faced with a dilemma. If they take a back seat, they run the risk, as exemplified in Devon and Cornwall, of inter-agency efforts failing to get off the ground or to keep going (Blaber, op.cit.; Moore and Brown, 1981). Furthermore the police are often better placed than anyone to know what the crime problems are and it would be unrealistic to deny that that they have the greatest incentive to do something about them. How far the police can legitimately go is, however, another question and one that can only be answered by appeal to a view of the practical and constitutional limits under which we wish them to operate. Deciding what the practical and constitutional limits to police participation should be is not easy. Theories of community policing which emphasise the proactive and preventive role of the police are of little help in reaching such a view.

There are other problems of multi-agency crime prevention which are to do with its effectiveness. As with community policing ideas about patrol, inter-agency cooperation has been seen as so self-evidently sensible, that relatively little attention has been paid to the difficulties of putting it into practice. As I have argued elsewhere (Weatheritt, 1986), coordinating the work of several organisations in order to prevent more crime is not only difficult to achieve but can also hinder effective action. This is because, even when they set out to act together, agencies do not always agree what the problems are, let alone how they should best be tackled. Even when a common understanding and agreed solutions can be arrived at, implementing those solutions may be difficult, time-consuming, costly or impossible (Hope and Murphy, 1983).

The problems of getting different organisations to work together are likely to be insignificant compared with those of increasing community cohesion and re-establishing lost informal social controls. What amounts to social engineering is also much more contentious than encouraging institutions to cooperate with one another. The role of the police in this process is more contentious still.

For John Alderson, moral entrepreneurship and moral leadership from the police are essential to the development of informal social control and hence fundamental to the police role. It is an interesting comment on the opaqueness of this vision that, although Alderson's theories have attracted criticism, his practice has on the whole been applauded (Baldwin and Kinsey, 1982, Chapter 8; Bradley, Walker and Wilkie, 1986, pp.110-113). Ironically, this may be because, stripped of its rhetoric, Alderson's practice was not readily distinguishable from that in many other forces. It involved the use of community constables (established practice in many forces since the 1960s and in rural forces long before that); schools liaison (pioneered in Sussex in the 1960s and again a well-established practice); and community consultation. In fact, Alderson's community hypothesis - that communities could be motivated to regulate themselves once stimulated to do so by police leadership, that this leadership would create informal social control where this was lacking and that this would lead to reductions in crime - remained largely untested by the practice in his force.

I have argued that community policing ideas require the police to expand and redefine their role in crime prevention. From being passive participants in a limited sphere, they are expected to move towards being equal partners or active participants in a more complex drama performed on a wider stage. These ideas are reflected in the development of official crime prevention policy and have also been used as a way of re-establishing the legitimacy of the police force. It is not just that more effective ways of preventing crime are being sought; a conscious attempt is also being made to improve the police image.

Involving the police in a wider range of activities and widening their role increases the problems which attach to that role. The more thoroughgoing versions of community policing raise fundamental questions about the proper limits to and scope of police activity. As currently formulated, community policing ideas fail either to acknowledge or to deal with these problems. Nor do theories of community policing carry within themselves the means to solve them. Whilst community policing ideas have been useful in stimulating debate and action, answers to policing problems cannot be found embedded in community policing philosophy nor in the practice to which it has given rise. This should come as no surprise. Controversy about the nature and sphere of police activity can only be settled by recourse to constitutional ideas about the police role which go far wider than crime or policing.

References

Alderson, J. (1979) *Policing Freedom*, Plymouth, Macdonald and Evans.

Baldwin, R. and Kinsey, R. (1982) *Police Powers and Politics*, London, Quartet Books.

Blaber, A. (1979) *The Exeter Community Policing Consultative Group: a study of the first year*, London, NACRO.

Bradley, D., Walker, N. and Wilkie, R. (1986) *Managing the Police: law, organisation and democracy*, Brighton, Wheatsheaf.

Brown, D. and Iles, S. (1985) *Community Constables: a study of a policing initiative*, Research and Planning Unit Paper 30, London, Home Office.

Clarke, R.V.G. and Hough, M. (1984) *Crime and Police Effectiveness*, Home Office Research Study 79, London, HMSO.

Clarke, R.V.G. and Mayhew, P. (editors) (1980) *Designing out Crime*, London, HMSO.

Ekblom, P. (1986) 'Community policing: obstacles and issues' in P. Willmott (editor) *The Debate About Community: papers from a seminar on Community in Social Policy*, Discussion Paper 13, London, Policy Studies Institute.

Ekblom, P. and Heal, K. (1982) *The Police Response to Calls from the Public*, Research and Planning Unit Paper 9, London, Home Office.

Hampshire Constabulary (1981) *The Havant Policing Scheme*. Unpublished report, Chief Constable's Office.

Hibberd, M. (1985) *The Colville Crime Survey: pre-test report on attitudes to crime and the police in a small area of Notting Hill*, London, Police Foundation.

Home Office (1967) 'Report of the working party on operational efficiency and management' in *Police Manpower, Equipment and Efficiency: reports of three working parties*, London, HMSO.

Hope, T. and Murphy, D.J.I. (1983) 'Problems of implementing crime prevention: the experience of a demonstration project', *Howard Journal*, vol.22, pp.38-50.

Jones, T., Maclean, B. and Young, J. (1986) *The Islington Crime Survey: crime, victimisation and policing in inner-city London*, Aldershot, Gower.

Kinsey, R. (1984) *Merseyside Crime Survey: first report, November 1984*, Merseyside County Council.

Moore, C. and Brown, J. (1981) *Community Versus Crime*, London, Bedford Square Press.

Moss, D.C. and Bucknall, R.A. (1983) *1982 Public Attitude Survey: report* and *Appendices*, Northamptonshire Police Management Services.

Smith, D. (1983) *Police and People in London. Volume I: a survey of Londoners*, London, Policy Studies Institute.

Smith, D. and Gray, J. (1983) *Police and People in London. Volume IV: the police in action*, London, Policy Studies Institute.

Southgate, P. and Ekblom, P. (1986) *Police-Public Encounters*, Home Office Research Study 90, London, HMSO.

Weatheritt, M. (1983) 'Community policing: does it work and how do we know?' in T. Bennett (editor) *The Future of Policing*, Cropwood Conference series 15, University of Cambridge.

Weatheritt, M. (1986) *Innovations in Policing*, London, Croom Helm.

West Midlands Police, (1982) *Resource Experiments, Volumes I and II*. Unpublished reports, Management Services Department.

3 POLICING BY THE PUBLIC AND POLICING BY THE POLICE

Joanna Shapland and Jon Vagg

A discussion of policing and the community presumes some knowledge of the nature of 'community'. However, the meaning of this term is notoriously variable and problematic (see, for example, Willmott, 1984). We hope to be forgiven for avoiding complex issues of definition by adopting a 'nose to the ground' approach in which we take community primarily to mean people's relationships to 'their' small geographical area and others in it. We shall look at residents' and business people's own views of the areas in which they live and work, the problems of order (in the 'law and order' sense) they perceive in those areas and the ways in which they deal with them, or want them dealt with by the police. To adapt a proposition of Bulmer's (1986) about community care: the formal and informal sides of social control may exist in an uneasy relation, in which policing by the police might easily undermine informal policing by the public - and the difference between a 'good' and 'bad' relationship between the two is probably that of a razor edge. This paper is about that proposition.

Much of what we say is based on our own research (Shapland and Vagg, 1985). We took a number of small areas from a shire county in the Midlands: a village (population 1,800) with a resident local police officer; a collection of small villages and hamlets (total population 1,600) policed from another village several miles away; and four small groups of streets ranging from the city centre of a county town (population 170,000) and the poorer housing surrounding it, out to the suburbs. All these areas contained a large amount of residential property, interspersed with shops, factories and other commercial premises. Our findings must obviously be specific to those areas, but, judging from the findings of attitudinal surveys such as the British Crime Survey and its more local equivalents (Hough and Mayhew, 1983; 1985; Jones, Maclean and Young, 1986; Kinsey, 1984), differences between areas would seem to be a matter of degree, rather than fundamental.

In order to map the incidents occurring in our areas and to study the views of residents, business people and police officers to them, we employed a wide variety of methods. By 'incidents' we mean occurrences of a wide range of events considered disturbing by residents and business people, for example public disorder, vandalism, noise, noisy or dangerous children's play, gangs of youths and suspicious-looking people. We interviewed a total of 322 residents and business people and 57 police officers in the areas, spent a total of 27 months informally observing (including 90 formal observation periods), and analysed a whole year of crime reports and 72 days of calls upon the police ('message pads'). The result was a mass of data on the problems and difficulties in the areas, including a log of all the incidents occurring over an 18-month period, together with attitudes towards them, the extent of knowledge about them and views on their resolution.

Problems and solutions
Within the broad category of disorder, it was clear that there were no distinctive kinds of problems that the police were called to deal with. Problems, in all areas, were by and large concerned with damage, teenagers 'hanging around', litter, noise, parked cars and the like. Our results regarding the calls by the public to the police for help concur with those of Ekblom and Heal (1982) in showing a wide spread of demands which are comparable with the types of problems cited by rural and urban residents in our study (and in others, such as Butler and Tharme's (1982) Chelmsley Wood survey).

Our study, however, shows that problem occurrences are very localised (often to one section of a street), and are also recurring. Whether an event would be cited as a problem related to how often it happened and how far the person concerned lived or worked from the place of its occurrence, not on the personal characteristics or attitudes of the person. However, the seriousness with which it would be viewed and the means for its solution were subject to enormous individual variation. In some urban areas, 'crime' also figured as a problem. About a quarter of all *incidents* our respondents told us about concerned things which were criminal - most typically, damage or theft. The view from the neighbourhood is predominantly not one of 'crime being committed' but of nuisance, problems and 'disorder' occurring.

People's impressions of how much disorder was occurring seemed to depend principally on how much they did *not* know rather than how much they did. The extent of knowledge about problematic incidents that had happened in the recent past was very patchy and almost as localised as the citing of events as problems. More importantly, the extent of worry about known problems or recent incidents depended upon who was thought to have done them. Those who saw damage or heard rowdyism and did not know who the culprits were, were most likely to be worried. Worry about problems, like fear of crime, is linked more to a fear of the unknown than to specific knowledge of nasty acts or people.

Solutions to problems are often difficult to find. A good parallel is Hawkins' (1984) comment on environmental regulation, where the problems for inspectors are often states of affairs such as dripping taps or unmended fences. Solutions can be found to the 'presenting problem' but the real issue is the underlying situation. In our study, the 'presenting problems' of disorder often disclosed underlying problems, such as a group of youths whose membership was loose knit and activities sporadic, and consequently as difficult to control as they were aggravating.

What did people do by way of informal policing? In both rural and urban areas, there was a large degree of watching/surveillance activity, much of it by the elderly and by business people, such as shop keepers, publicans, delivery people and odd job men. Where someone suspicious passed by, they would often be challenged indirectly, for example by asking if they were lost. The 'radius of watching' for suspicious people and things was very localised - a few houses or shops each way down the street.

'Radii of watching' - spatial areas over which a resident or business person habitually watches what is going on and will notice change - seem to be an important precondition for - if not an element of - informal social control. We would suggest that such spatial areas can always be drawn, though they may differ in size - that even in inner-city areas people watch their neighbours if nothing else. This watching area must, however, be distinguished from any sense of belonging to a 'community' or taking care of the property being observed. We asked all those we interviewed about their sense of belonging to 'their' local neighbourhood, however they defined this term. Predictably, urban dwellers showed much less sense of belonging (only 41 per cent said they felt they lived in a named and cohesive small part of the town and many of these did not agree on the name or the boundaries). And there was no correlation between someone feeling they belonged in this minimal way and their propensity to watch their neighbours. One may, after all, be equally nosy about people one distrusts or hates!

Taking action about a problem one observes will be a function of first having observed it and second being prepared to do something about it. One of the important concomitants of taking informal action appeared to be some sense of social obligation, for example to the owner of the property being attacked or feeling of responsibility in relation to it (such as being on a committee which was supposed to look after it). It is possible to posit a spatial area of social obligation, similar to the areas of watching, of the localisation of problems and of the extent of knowledge about problems we mentioned above. Of these, it would seem that watching is the most localised, followed by problem identification and knowledge. A chart of one person's 'spatial areas of social obligation' may of course be confined to any one area; it may be centred principally around the person's house but also encompass, say, the houses of friends living at a distance. All, however, are far smaller than any idea of 'community' or named areas within cities or villages.

Watching was very prevalent, but further action was far more variable, depending upon the culprit and the nature of the locality. The wrongdoing might be broadcast on the grapevine, so that the culprit would (hopefully) know that others were aware of it. People might be accosted directly and perhaps asked for compensation. The threat of involving the police might be used; or the culprit might be punished in some appropriate way - a person who often caused parking problems had his car 'boxed in' by others. If all else failed, 'target hardening' might be done - concreting-in litter bins and the like. As a general rule, no further action was taken by neighbours or sympathisers without it being agreed by the victim.

Some action was taken, however, which had the flavour of both social control and community care. In the rural area, people would 'adopt' areas such as the verges outside their homes, and keep them tidy; damage would be made good quickly. This recalls the suggestion - unfortunately never fully substantiated - of studies such as Power (1982) that quick repair may actually deter further vandalism.

Damage to telephone boxes, street lights and the like were sometimes discussed in parish council meetings, and council members were expected to intervene if they saw anything suspicious happening by such property. However, while parish councils might 'target harden' (by concreting-in litter bins or installing toughened glass in notice boards) or write letters to individuals against whom a substantial complaint could be laid, their lack of powers ensured that the police were often held to be the only viable alternative. In the urban areas matters were more clear cut since councils of an equivalent size to parish councils do not exist, and 'responsible local persons' such as local teachers and others who could be intermediaries in social control are similarly absent. Individuals would deal with matters themselves if they thought it possible or appropriate (if for example the culprit lived nearby) or they would involve the police. The police tended to be called more often and to more trivial incidents in the urban areas.

Police roles and informal action
We have said very little so far about the role of the police in our areas - but their presence or absence, kinds of responses and attitudes were very important in determining the overall pattern of social control even though they did not appear to have the degree of absolute control over the definition and resolution of disorder that they might have liked. Residents and business people would decide whether to call in the police (the decision usually being left to the victim, unless 'real crime' - burglaries of dwellings, physical and sexual attacks - was concerned). The police also tended to be called when informal strategies could not, or did not, work - an event more common in the urban than rural areas given the lack of a 'middle range' of informal options. The problem became 'police property' rather than 'private property' in Nils Christie's (1977) sense of the term. Control of 'what would happen next' passed from the complainant to the police and it was very rare that any information about what was decided would be passed back to the victim or others in the area.

There is probably some truth in Holdaway's (1983) suggestion that police see the public as 'chaotic' and disorganised. They are required to offer 'a rough and ready way of dealing quickly and cheaply with a large throughput of people's problems' (Ekblom, 1986). However, their distinctive feature in doing this is that they have a monopoly on the legitimate use of force, and consequently a strong hand in 'defining' situations they attend. Perhaps this is the crux of the matter; the police might be said to have an operational philosophy that their role is to make situations controllable and manipulable (because the public cannot), and so they attempt to develop strategies for achieving this. Where serious crime is concerned, the public may accept or even demand that the police 'take over' in this way. Few were overtly bothered by having their burglary, for example, dealt with by an anonymous officer.

But there may be a low-level 'battle' between police and citizen for control of what should happen in other, more minor instances. The vast majority of incidents or problems will not be seen as serious crimes by the public (though they will be seen as wrong and may involve a breach of the criminal law, such as instances of vandalism or theft). In many of these cases we found victims, complainants and witnesses wishing to know what had happened, and some who wished to have some input into subsequent decisions. Especially where local issues and personalities were involved, it became important to know whether the policemen dealing with the situation would attach weight to local feelings about the incident. People used various strategems to try and ensure this. One of our interviewees, for example, a victim of stones thrown at a window, had several arguments with various officers sent to take statements, etc, and effectively stopped a charge being brought against the juvenile responsible - at the cost of a great deal of effort on her part. And people who knew one or other of the area beat officers would tend to wait until they came past in order to raise non-urgent matters, rather than risk an unknown policeman dealing with the matter.

Another potential point of dispute between public and police arises from the trite but true observation that police officers always describe themselves and think of themselves as being called to incidents rather than problems. For many officers, and certainly to the controllers/dispatchers who assign jobs to officers, pieces of work are to be attended, solved and finished with - preferably within that shift. They have great difficulty, as does the police information system, in dealing with the recurring but localised problems that form so much of the demands of the public.

This summary of police attitudes, however, masks the divergence of perspective between officers doing different jobs, or with different attitudes to what is good police work. We would argue that there is not a single occupational culture (as, for example, Holdaway (1983) has suggested). We found a diversity of views as to how incidents and complainants should be dealt with. In our areas, broadly speaking, the area beat officers were involved in many of the routine inquiries and summonses and minor crimes, liked to feel that they had a unique overview of their patch, and were prepared to spend time to track down persistent nuisances and criminals. However, they did not have the means (for example a desk at the station, a means of being contacted direct by the public) to collate and pass on the often trivial information about gangs, minor damage and the like which could lead to an overview of a problem (as opposed to dealing with instances of its occurrence). Moreover, they were often organisationally distanced from other police officers by such basic considerations as shift patterns. Immediate response car crews tended to value the element of police work which is about a speedy, professional response, particularly to serious emergencies, and a 'quick in, quick out' approach. And CID officers tended to operate separately from (even though formally they were expected to liaise with) other officers. They were in some sense a 'soak' for crimes such as burglary, for which the area officers might feel their local knowledge could be helpful. There was, however, rarely effective liaison, let alone joint working on such crimes, except in areas which had adopted a territorial team approach including CID officers.

Senior ranks have, yet again, a slightly different set of priorities. They are often concerned to improve community relations and to find schemes and solutions which do address problems at the core. Hence they promote projects such as neighbourhood watch. Similarly, in one area we studied, the superintendent was looking at ways of reducing complaints about parking problems and had contacted the local authority with a view to changing the street layout (kerb height, flower tubs, etc). But despite all this, one constraint on community and neighbourhood policies is clear. Senior police managers work with local authorities, residents' associations, youth clubs and the like. Yet many organisations are not 'local enough' to deal effectively with (or even know about) neighbourhood issues and problems, or have a partisan interest in their resolution.

Divergences of views

We have suggested that the view from the street is one of residents experiencing 'disorder', 'watching out' for suspicious or problematic things, but finding that the police on the ground expect trouble to be 'handed over' while dealing with each occurrence of a problem as an isolated incident. On the other hand, the 'problem management' view is employed by senior police, who, however, operate at a level of formal committees where local neighbourhood problems are not raised, or where most of their contact may be with, in Eldon Griffith's phrase, the great and the good (Morgan and Maggs, 1985) rather than those, like small shopkeepers or the elderly, who may be more 'plugged in' to the informal networks.

What did people want from the police? A large majority of those we interviewed wanted to know the police officers they were dealing with, what they could expect from them, and how police action might be influenced when influence was wanted. However, the people who see the police comparatively rarely are those who have no wish to call on their services and who are not suspicious of them, a group which includes many of the 'watchers' in the informal network.

'Good' and 'bad' police-public relations

The police are perhaps not fully aware that they do not constitute the only, or even necessarily the major, source of social control. Public wishes are for the police to play certain parts at certain times. Currently, police organisation, supervision and provision of administrative support can often be unhelpful to the best performance of these roles. The present concentration on the best means of consultation with the community, although a very worthy and useful aim in itself, cannot produce the solution to these problems, simply because consultation is an approximate science. The methods used tend to rely on organisations and committees. Yet such bodies are only partly lodged within neighbourhoods and communities and have different priorities from those of people at large.

It seems to us that the ultimate aim of good police-public relations is one which can only be worked out on the ground. It means having police on the beat who are known to the right sections of the public - including those who watch. It means collecting and using apparently casually-offered clues as to what people expect from their policeman and from the police generally. We are not implying a Wilson and Kelling (1982) style approach, in which beat officers are expected to enforce 'neighbourhood rules' such as keeping drunks away from bus stops. We do not propose that the police should necessarily or automatically adopt any such rules as may exist, merely that they should be able and prepared to articulate the basis on which they are policing that area. More importantly for the English context, we did not find that such rules existed. Opinion was normally very divided as to the seriousness of problems and the methods to be used to deal with them. Where, rarely, there was relative unanimity, it tended to relate to the predictability (or unpredictability) of police action rather than to substantive social-control issues.

Bad relations may come in a variety of forms. Unfortunately some current operational strategies may inadvertently promote them. There is a police tendency to 'deal with incidents' by taking them over, to deploy officers so that they are relatively unknown to those living or working on the beats they patrol and not to foster local knowledge, so losing contact with the informal network. If 'community options' are then bolted on, as Ekblom has noted, a lack of police-public interaction may become a community means of keeping an unwanted police intrusion at bay. At the other extreme, to end with another adaptation from Bulmer, the police may try - or be invited - to 'colonise' informal watching mechanisms by, say, introducing neighbourhood watch. But were this to be done without also attaching more weight to what the watchers want done, they are likely to be replacing a working informal mechanism by a failing formal one.

* * * * * *

The authors' research, on which this paper is based, was funded by the Home Office. The views expressed are those of the authors.

References
Bulmer, M. (1986) *Neighbours: the work of Philip Abrams*, Cambridge, Cambridge University Press.
Butler, A.J.P. and Tharme, K. (1982) *Social Survey: Chelmsley Wood Sub-Division*. Unpublished, West Midlands Police.
Christie, N. (1977) 'Conflicts as property', *British Journal of Criminology*, vol 17, pp 1-15.
Ekblom, P. (1986) 'Community policing: obstacles and issues', in P. Willmott, (editor) *The Debate About Community: papers from a seminar on Community in Social Policy*, Discussion Paper 13, London, Policy Studies Institute.
Ekblom, P. and Heal, K. (1982) *The Police Response to Calls From the Public*, Research and Planning Unit Paper 9, London, Home Office.
Hawkins, K. (1984) *Environment and Enforcement*, Oxford, Oxford University Press.
Holdaway, D. (1983) *Inside the British Police*, Oxford, Basil Blackwell.
Hough, M. and Mayhew, P, (1983) *The British Crime Survey: first report*, Home Office Research Study 76, London, HMSO.

Hough, M. and Mayhew, P. (1985) *Taking Account of Crime: key findings from the second British Crime Survey*, Home Office Research Study 85, London, HMSO.

Jones, T., Maclean, B. and Young, Y. (1986) *The Islington Crime Survey: crime, victimisation and policing in inner-city London*, Aldershot, Gower.

Kinsey, R. (1984) *Merseyside Crime Survey: first report*, Liverpool, Police Committee Support Unit.

Morgan, R. and Maggs, C. (1985) *Setting the PACE: police community consultation arrangements in England and Wales*, Bath Social Policy Papers 4, Bath, University of Bath.

Power, A. (1982) *Priority Estates Project 1982. Improving Problem Council Estates: a summary of aims and progress*, London, Department of the Environment.

Shapland, J. and Vagg, J. (1985) *Social Control and Policing in Rural and Urban Areas*. Unpublished report, Oxford, Centre for Criminological Research.

Willmott, P. (1984) *Community in Social Policy*, Discussion Paper 9, London, Policy Studies Institute.

Wilson, J.Q. and Kelling, G.L. (1982) 'Broken windows: the police and neighbourhood safety', *The Atlantic Monthly*, March, pp 29-38.

4 THE LOCAL DETERMINANTS OF POLICING POLICY

Rod Morgan

'There is one important fact we should never forget', the superintendent said at a police community consultative meeting I attended recently. 'There is no such thing as the British police. There are 43 quite separate police forces in England and Wales. It is not relevant for us to talk here about what the police do in London or Birmingham or Manchester. Here in Middleshire we do things our own way. We have our own Force and the policies of the Middleshire Constabulary are, we believe, suited to what the Middleshire people expect and want.'

Though correct *de jure*, the *de facto* validity of the superintendent's opening statement is widely contested. There are 43 separate police forces. All of them, outside London, are subject to the divided but shared responsibilities of their chief constables, local police authorities and the Home Secretary, the so-called tripartite structure of the Police Act 1964. However, it is generally agreed that the distribution of power within the tripartite structure has shifted markedly in recent years from the police authorities to the Association of Chief Police Officers (ACPO) and the Home Office (Spencer, 1985). Events during and since the miners' strike have led some commentators to argue that we have a national police force in all but name (Fine and Millar, 1985). Further, so many observers maintain, the police, by virtue of force amalgamations, increased reliance on technology and greater specialisation, are, as Lord Scarman put it, in danger of becoming 'a *corps d'elite* set apart from the rest of the community' (1981, para. 5.3). They have, it is argued by some, become out of touch with the public, using methods which do not command community support and pursuing objectives and priorities which are not those of the citizens they allegedly serve (Kinsey, Lea and Young, 1986).

For these reasons 'police accountability' is a high profile issue, the subject of intense party political controversy (Reiner, 1985). Advocates on the left favour radical constitutional reform to create a locally elected police authority for London and to grant all local police committees the power to determine aspects of police policy which have hitherto been held to be the prerogative of chief constables (Lustgarten, 1986). The Conservative government is committed to retain the tripartite structure. However, as we shall see, the government is welding to it initiatives designed to maintain or restore the partnership between police and community which, it is argued, has always been the hallmark of

British 'policing by consent'. It is against this background that I want to consider whether, as a result of these recent initiatives, it can reasonably be claimed that the people of Middleshire do get policing which is sensitive to their needs and, just as importantly, whether they can know they are getting it.

Background: aims and resources
We need to begin with a few words about relationships and resources. As a result of claims that services throughout the public sector are insufficiently attuned to consumer interests, it is fashionable to argue for their decentralisation (Stewart, Deakin and Wright, 1984; Smith, 1985). Decentralisation, however, can take the form of local administration as well as local government (Widdicombe, 1986). Advocates of professional as well as political accountability systems hold out the promise of greater sensitivity to consumers (see Kogan, 1986) and decentralisation may involve parallel initiatives in local government and local administration (see Collingridge, 1986). Because of well-rehearsed constitutional controversies, discussions of policing have focussed on the framework for political accountability but have had relatively little to say about local administration and the manner in which professional accountability is or might be wedded to it.

The most important level of local administration in policing is the sub-division. Normally covering a population between 60,000 and 150,000, the sub-division is the basic unit for day-to-day operational team work and decision making. Ecologically, sub-divisions vary enormously. So also do their resources and organisation. Though each police force has a manpower establishment fixed by the Home Office, and though each force develops its own approach to such matters as functional specialisation and command and control, the differences between sub-divisions are arguably greater than the differences between forces. Broadly speaking it is the character of the sub-division which determines what service the public receives locally.

There is no agreed magic formula which, mechanically applied, determines what resources a sub-division gets. The manpower reviews which most forces periodically undertake tend increasingly to be under-pinned by the application of a number of input and output criteria. Some criteria assume demand for policing - the population of the sub-division or the number of miles of Class A roads it contains. Other criteria are based on actual demands - the number of logged messages, crimes recorded or gun licences issued. And others are based on outputs - the numbers of prisoners held, persons proceeded against, etc. These criteria are incommensurable, however, and there is no agreement as to what weight should be given to each. In the final analysis what resources a sub-division gets is a mixture of precedent and argument about current workloads. Among police officers the argument is fierce and continuous because all know that the indicators have a circular quality: the demands made on the police reflect public expectations locally, which in turn are determined partly by the quality of the existing service and relations with the police.

Whatever the shortcomings of such measures, the police can reasonably claim that, within the constraints dictated nationally, the allocation of resources and the quality of policing locally are substantially determined by the character of each area and the demands which consumers make directly on the police through phone calls and visits to stations. Moreover, resource allocation decisions within sub-divisions - the number of beats and their coverage, the retention of sub-stations and the number of hours they are open, etc. - are made in much the same manner. What the police have hitherto generally failed to do, however, is to reveal, at neighbourhood, sub-division or police authority level, the basis on which they determine resource allocation. Thus the manner and degree to which localities determine the policing they receive is largely unknown outside the police. It remains an open question, therefore, whether local politicians or other community representatives would endorse the local administrative conclusions to which the police come. This is vital because the ratio of police officers to population is substantially higher, as much as twice as high, in some areas compared to others.

Current orthodoxy in the Home Office is that these aspects of policy should be more open to public scrutiny and, more importantly, that despite their retention of operational autonomy the police should engage in a *partnership* with the community for making local policy. To those who seek *political accountability* of the police to local police committees (meaning operational control of the police by committees), the government argues that, instead, the police will develop their *professional accountability* best by demonstrating their sensitivity to consumer interests and making transparent their operational decisions. This professionalism has three components. Greater bureaucratisation regarding routine decision-making (legal accountability), and centralisation regarding such matters as mutual aid arragements, equipment and service standards (administrative accountability), will be dovetailed to greater devolution of operational planning (managerial accountability). Increased professionalism, it is argued, will therefore safeguard standards of service whilst maximising sensitivity to citizens' interests locally.

Several initiatives give substance to these claims:
- Section 106 of the Police and Criminal Evidence Act 1984 requires that arrangements be made in each area for obtaining the views of people about matters concerning the policing of their area. As a result of Home Office Circulars this provision has been interpreted almost everywhere to mean the setting up of police community consultative committees by sub-division (Morgan and Maggs, 1985; Morgan, 1986).
- The application of the government's 'financial management initiative' (FMI) to policing. This has resulted in the search for police performance indicators, the development of methods for more systematic appraisal of forces by Her Majesty's Inspectorate of Constabulary (HMI), and the specification of aims and methods for assessing their achievement within forces (see, for example, Chief Constable of Merseyside, 1986): the current vogue for 'policing by objectives' flows from this. The government has indicated that these aids to more effective management should be shared with police authorities in deciding bids for more resources (see Home Office Circular 114/1983).
- The encouragement by the Home Office of liaison between different

statutory services locally to develop joint crime prevention planning (Home Office Circular 8/1984).

- The introduction of schemes for lay visitors to police stations, whereby nominated persons pay unannounced visits to stations to inspect conditions, check the custody records the police are now obliged to keep and make themselves available to prisoners wishing to complain about the conditions of their custody (Home Office Circular 12/1986).

Taken together these initiatives are designed to reinforce the doctrine of legal accountability, bolster the tripartite arrangements for the governance of the police, and breathe life back into the proposition that locally, particularly in the inner city areas which have witnessed violent confrontations between the police and sections of the public since 1980, there is 'policing by consent'. I want to spend the rest of this paper considering the likely impact of one of these initiatives - police/community consultation - for enhancing the degree to which police policy locally is sensitive to public needs.

The original rationale for local consultation, outlined first by Lord Scarman and subsequently endorsed in Home Office Circulars, is that police *efficiency* is dependent on police and public notions of police *effectiveness* being congruent. The argument is that the police only know about and solve most crime because the public choose to tell them 'who done what'. This vital flow of information is best safeguarded by the police being attuned to public concerns: consultation, it is maintained, will ensure that the police are not out of touch with what it is the public wants. Consultation will also enable the police to educate the public as to the limitations of the service they are able to provide and, having demonstrated they are pursuing common objectives, can also be used to mobilise the public to assist the police in practical ways or engage in various self-help operations.

The view that acceptable and effective policing depends crucially on mutual police/public confidence and cooperation is held as much by those on the left as the right of the political spectrum. Many left-wing critics also advocate the establishment of local consultative mechanisms (Downes and Ward, 1986; Kinsey, Lea and Young, 1986; Cox, 1986). There is a fundamental difference between left and right on this question however. Whereas the government has introduced consultation as an adjunct to the existing framework of constabulary independence - consultation without power and formal political accountability - those on the left seek consultation within a system of elected local authority control over police policy. Indeed many left-wing critics dismiss the current consultative arrangements as a public relations charade (Scraton, 1985; Spencer, 1985).

There is one final scene-setting point of which we should take note. There is a group of analysts of police policy who take a more complex and less overtly partisan view of consultation. These commentators are sceptical of the degree to which accountability, thought of in the very broadest sense of congruence between police and community regarding priorities and values (Bayley, 1983), is achieved simply by either legal rules or formal systems of political accountability (see Savage, 1984; Reiner, 1985; Smith, 1986). They stress the need for checks and balances, creating points for dialogue and making policy visible, developing systems which will lead the police to open rather than close ranks. Seen from this perspective, consultation, whatever form it takes, is no panacea for the ills from which it arose, but may nevertheless serve as a positive link in the chain of acceptable policing.

Police community consultative committees

Though there is variation in the way Section 106 of the 1984 Act is being interpreted in different parts of the country, the following generalisations cover the arrangements typical of most areas:

- All but one or two of the 43 police authorities in England and Wales have set up formal police community consultative committees with force-wide constitutions and terms of reference closely modelled on Home Office Circulars 54/1982 and 2/1985.
- Consultative committees are in most cases based on police sub-divisions rather than local authority areas: this emphasises police local administration rather than the political accountability of local government. (In the Metropolitan Police District, where there is no locally elected police authority, consultation has been based on boroughs as a gesture towards local government.)
- Committees generally meet quarterly, are chaired by elected members of the police authority (though not in London where there is no locally elected police authority) and typically have 15 to 25 members appointed partly or wholly by the police authority.
- Committees usually meet in local authority or neighbourhood premises rather than police stations, and invariably make provision for parts of meetings, or occasional meetings, to be open to the public. The publicity for meetings is generally poor.
- The membership of committees typically includes representatives of: county district and parish councils; the principal statutory services (invariably education and youth services, sometimes social services, housing, leisure, probation, etc.); the churches; trades councils and/or chambers of commerce; ethnic minority organisations; residents' and tenants' associations; neighbourhood action groups; and voluntary service organisations, particularly those for the aged. The police, if not actually members, are most usually represented by the sub-divisional superintendent and attend as of right.
- Committee members are seldom under 30 years of age and typically are active 'respectable' members of the community. They *represent* one organisation and are usually involved in others. Generally speaking, they are *not* the sort of people who have previously had much contact with the police (except possibly socially) and, though they know little of the police, are invariably well-disposed towards them. They are not generally people who have been in conflict with the police or have adverse personal experience of them. Groups hostile to the police typically dismiss consultative committees as a meaningless charade on the grounds that they lack power and are merely for public relations; such groups often refuse to be involved.

- Very few forces provide committees with any back-up staff and where support is provided it is usually only to assist with arrangements for fixing venues, taking minutes, sending out invitations, etc. Most committees are provided with no more than a small annual budget to cover the hire of halls, postage, etc. Consultative committees, like their parent police authorities, generally have no independent expert/research support.

There are conspicuous exceptions to this picture. Some areas, like Lambeth and Merseyside, have 'forum' type committees; membership is open to all local organisations and meetings are public and much more frequent. In a few areas, the members of committees can seek the assistance of police monitoring groups who collect data independently of the police and acquire expertise regarding police procedures and policies. These conditions are rare.

Committee dynamics

The life of the typical consultative committee follows a pattern. Early meetings are dominated by constitutional questions, finding and appointing members, deciding the format of meetings, determining what part non-members can play. The sub-divisional commander is generally invited to describe his patch and the manner in which he polices it. If the committee adopts a 'travelling circus' approach, holding public meetings in different neighbourhoods, the superintendent is likely to be asked to do his basic presentation repeatedly. Most committee meetings thereafter revolve around the report of the commander or a specially invited police guest: crime prevention, schools liaison and drugs specialists are favourites.

Superintendents generally outline the geography of their sub-divisions, describe the headquarters and any sub-stations and explain the beat system. They typically say how many officers and cars they have at their disposal and, with different degrees of precision, run through their allocation of staff by area and function. Having gone through the business of shifts, rest days, mutual aid, training and the growing paperwork demands placed on them, they frequently inform their audiences how many constables can normally be deployed, on foot, in the sub-division at any one time during the day. In the space of a few clinical minutes audiences, many of whose members will subsequently say they want to see more officers patrolling their neighbourhoods, are told that an allocation of approximately 100 officers to the sub-division actually means there are only five or six to go out on patrol simultaneously. Though informative, these pictures of police resources are often misleading and ahistorical: they almost always ignore civilian, headquarters and other specialist or support staff and they tend to suggest a past golden age.

Officers typically transmit two other messages. First, that the demands made on the police are outstripping the resources available to them. Crime is rising, the bureaucratic requirements growing ever more burdensome, public expectations of the police expanding and, thus, the need to ration what the police do becoming ever more imperative. An illustration is commonly provided by talking about the 'graded response' system which many forces are currently introducing. The impression conveyed is that the police are being engulfed. Secondly, insofar as officers talk about a particular aspect of the demands placed on them, it is the growing incidence of serious crime. If statistics are produced they are invariably of burglary and violent crime. If anecdotal accounts of incidents are offered they usually concern indictable offences of the sort which, if prosecuted, would be committed to crown courts.

These police accounts provide the centrepiece for most consultative committee discussions, public or closed. They are reinforced by organised visits to police stations and are supplemented by talks from local beat or specialist officers. Consultative committee meetings often look like WEA classes in policing. Audiences are appreciative. Being little acquainted with policing and having minimal personal or indirect experience of serious crime, they find the information interesting and alarming. People are surprised there are so few officers on the ground. They are disturbed to find the police so overwhelmed by problems which appear to demand a police response. Committee members, already well disposed towards the police, now report they are better informed about what the police do and more sympathetic to police problems. They want to help.

When given the opportunity to say something, members are as likely to ask questions of the superintendent, seeking more information about police organisation and procedures, as they are to describe the local problems they encounter or comment on the police service they get. Their expression of the consumer's standpoint becomes interwoven with their education as to what service they can expect the police to deliver. For, unlike the police, they generally (though this varies from area to area) do *not* talk about serious crimes. Apart from the reassuring presence of more foot patrols, typically they want the police to do something about nuisances, incivilities and inconveniences. Traffic problems - speeding, parking, abandoned vehicles and the absence of pedestrian crossings - figure prominently. The behaviour of youths - their noise, their intimidatory street corner habits, their cycles on footpaths, their motor bike racing, their foul language, graffiti and minor acts of vandalism - are perennial topics. And the quality of the environment - litter, dog-shit, uneven pavements, poor street lighting, uncollected rubbish, unrepaired street furniture, insecure council housing fittings - these are the matters members raise and about which they seek action.

Though many of these environmental problems are not directly the responsibility of the police, it is nevertheless often useful to discuss them at police consultative committee meetings. There are usually councillors and sometimes local government officers present with direct responsibility for the services complained of. But as far as policing is concerned, the requests for action tend to bounce back on the complainants. Even when the police have a responsibility, what more can they do? Given their accounts of serious crime it begins to seem reasonable to audiences that the police should give low priority to such matters as youths cycling on footpaths. Clearly it is sensible that the police should respond urgently to disturbances in progress rather than burglaries several hours old. Nor, given the myriad demands apparently made on the police locally and elsewhere, does there any longer seem much prospect that the local constable will be able to spend more than the low proportion of time he currently does on his 'permanent' beat.

Unless, of course, there were more police officers: committee members are by now convinced there should be. That the police do not have more officers is not, it emerges, the fault of the police. Superintendents and councillors representing all political parties quickly remind their audiences that the authorised establishment for the Middleshire Constabulary is determined by the Home Office. More officers have been requested, but the request has been refused or only partly met. In the short term, the most that can be done is for the county councillor chairman to argue at the police authority that the sub-division should get a larger slice of the force's cake. Sub-divisional superintendents, needless to say, are well pleased that the poverty of their local empires will be criticised passionately in other forums.

To describe consultative committees in these terms is not to suggest that they have no useful practical outcomes for neighbourhoods. Councillors, the police and the representatives of other statutory services do, jointly, have their attention focussed on local problems and action sometimes results. Participants sometimes report that the committee played a part in getting a traffic layout altered, a section of poor street lighting improved, an inefficient local constable transferred or the licence for a troublesome public house taken away. It is possible that many of these complaints would have been registered and remedies found through the use of informal consultative methods in place before committees were introduced. That is not necessarily the point. Committees are now being used and, more importantly, are increasingly likely to provide an institutional framework to which persons and groups without informal links with the police can resort. Yet though committees are clearly fulfilling consumer articulation and educational functions, a question mark hangs over the quality of that education. The portrayal of policing is partial, simplistic and rose-tinted. The demand for more police officers is fuelled without questioning the assumption that more will mean a better service or a safer society. And seldom is any doubt expressed that the way policing is currently conducted is other than it should or could be.

Given the publicity which attends rows between a few chief constables and local politicians this portrayal of consultative committees will no doubt seem astonishing. But it is so. Around the country, at regular consultative meetings, heads are nodding in agreement. My concern is to draw attention to the superficiality of this public education on policing. It is a theme to which I shall return.

There is one other, better publicised, aspect of committee work to which I need briefly to refer. Lord Scarman originally expressed the view that consultative committees might constructively be involved in the planning of police operational policy, though he recognised this could not always be done (1981, para 5.56). The proposition initially received little encouragement from the police or the Home Office. The first Circular on consultation dealt with the question negatively by stressing the circumstances under which it would be wrong to discuss operational matters (Home Office Circular 54/1982). By 1985 the Home Office had adopted a more positive tone: 'the police should be as open as possible ... ready to discuss all aspects of police aims and policy including operational matters and the outcomes of complaints investigations'

(Home Office Circular 2/1985).

From a police standpoint the benefits of this approach were dramatically illustrated in Brixton in 1985. Whereas 'Swamp 81', in combination with a breakdown of police consultation with community groups locally, provided the precipitating backcloth to the 1981 Brixton disturbances, 'Swamp 85' was mounted with the approval of the Lambeth Police Community Consultative Committee. More recently, in St Paul's Bristol in September 1986, the police justified their well organised and massively reinforced raids on several addresses for the stated purpose of discovering drugs, by referring to pressure for action received from local consultative groups. On the evening of the day the raids were carried out, as the neighbourhood flared with incidents of stone throwing and petrol bombing, senior oficers and 'community leaders', including the white chairperson of the sub-divisional consultative committee (who was also chair of the police authority) and the black chairperson of an informal consultative group for the St Paul's neighbourhood itself, supported the police operation as a necessary crack-down on a criminal minority.

In both the Brixton and Bristol examples the 'community leaders' on the consultative committees were subsequently disowned by other neighbourhood 'spokespersons' (the chair of the Avon and Somerset Police Authority was forced to resign by his Labour colleagues). The committees were alleged to be unrepresentative, their members to have no credibility locally. Police operations were variously described as unnecessary, provocative, heavy handed and racist. Nevertheless, in both cases and despite serious disorders, the police were able publicly to justify their actions on the grounds that they were taken in the interests and at the behest of the neighbourhoods they entered in strength. 'Community leaders' spoke up to legitimate the operations. Of course critics still described the police as external oppressors. But they were unable to do so without contradiction - not, as previously, from the police or 'outsiders' (including government ministers) but from local residents.

Whatever the rights and wrongs of these police operations, however representative or unrepresentative the 'community leaders' and 'spokespersons', the moral and political status of the police position had been transformed by the existence of formal consultative procedures. It was no longer plausible for commentators to present an argument simply in terms of the police *against* the community. The debate was now firmly *within* the community, where those critics who press for greater police accountability repeatedly maintain it should be. The question at issue, however, is whether this shift represents an apparent or a substantive shift of the basis on which police operational decisions are or should be taken.

Consultation: problems and prospects

In most parts of the country the question of community involvement in the planning of police operational policy as yet scarcely arises. Spectacular police operations of the Brixton and St Paul's type are not relevant simply because they so seldom happen. More importantly, routine operational policy is not discussed in any meaningful sense because, as has been shown, the sort of people who attend consultative committees generally have little or no experience of policing and, possessing only that information which the police choose to give them, are persuaded that the police do the best they can with limited resources. Committees do not *discuss* operational policy because they peceive there to be little to discuss. Their members generally have no grounds on which to disapprove of what the police do. Typically they are not victims of serious crime, police inaction or malpractice. They have no burning desire to discover alternative methods by which their neighbourhoods might be policed. And, understandably, the police let satisfied sleeping dogs lie: they do not present members with operational choices nor do they reveal the different options they have at their disposal.

The few consultative committees that wish to probe operational policy suffer from handicaps structured by this national picture. Like any profession or organisation, the police explain themselves best when they are able to do so in a broadly supportive atmosphere. Currently, however, external analysis of police operational policy invariably coincides with controversial and highly charged settings. For this to change, public analysis of operational policy has to become a normal undertaking, a routine discussion. At present probing questions are usually interpreted by the police, quite accurately in many circumstances, as critical. This hostile climate, which results in defensiveness on the part of the police and coincides with belligerency on the part of critics, is damaging in the extreme for police/community relations.

It would be naive to suggest that no problems would attend public discussion of operational policy were it to be conducted routinely in calmer environs. There are intrinsic difficulties which will only be overcome with mutual goodwill and understanding. First, from a police standpoint the discussion of operational options involves certain pitfalls. It means revealing something about how police discretion is or might be exercised. This leaves the police open to potential attack. For example, the balance struck between law enforcement and the maintenance of public tranquility does not, as is sometimes sensationally claimed, lead to the creation of 'no go' areas. But it does mean there are 'go slow' neighbourhoods, areas where the police do not rush in. Or it leads to 'stop-go' policing, the adoption of a low profile approach with occasional major operations, as in Bristol. Revealing their local informal operational rules may in the short term lead the police to be acted against legally (see, for example, *Regina v Oxford ex part Levey, Times Law Report*, 18 December 1985) or criticised publicly. There is no shortage of local politicians ready to pounce on evidence of anything short of strict law enforcement to accuse the police of discrimination, partiality or failure to uphold their legal duty. The current framework for the governance of the police, within which councillors have no political responsibility for operational policy, actually encourages their taking one-sided or parochial stances regarding it.

Further, in the long term, such revelations may undermine the police case for retention of operational autonomy. For insofar as the police frame and disclose rules as to when, how and why the law should be enforced selectively, or set themselves objectives in advance as opposed to acting reactively and contingently, their case for not submitting to operational political control is vitiated (see Waddington, 1986). The whole basis of the case for increased political accountability is that the law offers the police no guidance as to how they should exercise their unavoidable discretion and that, in consequence, police policy is as much political as legal (Baldwin and Kinsey, 1982; Lustgarten, 1986).

Second, because the majority of police authority and consultative committee members are satisfied with the service the police give and are content to leave the job to the 'professionals', those members who seek information about operational policy are unusual and tend to be marginalised by their fellow politicians, the media and the police. They are referred to as trouble makers. They are described, quite meaninglessly, as 'politically motivated', as if the decision *not* to call the police to account amounted to political impartiality or squared better with democracy, whereas of course it does neither. It follows that the perception of these members and committees as 'troublesome' both feeds police fears about the motives behind operational questions and makes it easier for them to resist providing answers. The consequence, despite the exhortations of the Home Office, is to encourage conservatism and paranoia on the part of the police. Thus, for example, some consultative committees are denied written reports from the police, or are refused crime statistics or achieved manning levels for particular neighbourhoods. Data that could and probably should be treated as routine, serving as a basis for constructive discussion, are rendered controversial. Fears that information will be misused, taken out of context, are increased and possibly well founded largely because the information is not part of a normal context.

Third, the passive non-inquiring posture adopted by most members towards operational matters means they see no need to gain expertise about the service. Only a handful of police authorities have created independent mechanisms for briefing or servicing either themselves or their consultative committee members. It follows that members seldom have information about the police other than what the police choose to give them. Inquiring members are therefore relatively rudderless, unable satisfactorily to penetrate the police bureaucracy and vulnerable to the charge that at best their questions betray a lack of understanding or at worst are motivated by malice. The system reinforces the ignorance or bad intentions of which inquiring members are subsequently accused.

Conclusions and prescriptions
The argument and evidence in this paper concern the relationship between political and professional systems of accountability and the sensitivity of police services to consumers locally. The principal points are as follows. The police are not subject to political control of operational policy locally. Their claim to continued operational autonomy is, however, being nurtured by appeals to greater professionalism, including devolved local administration and accountability to consumers. The introduction of consultative committees by sub-division is a major part of the institutional framework within which these processes supposedly operate and are made visible.

Consultative committees are almost everywhere in place and are proving to

have limited practical value to neighbourhoods. They provide a forum for the
ventilation of local problems and sometimes serve as the mechanism for forging
practical solutions agreed between the police, community groups, local
politicians and other statutory services. However, the principal determinants of
the quantity and quality of police services locally - manpower allocation, the
relationship between uniformed and specialist branches, the provision and
deployment of equipment, decisions about priorities and police tactics, etc -
though decided by police managers on the basis of indices of alleged consumer
needs and demands are, for the most part, fixed centrally (within force
headquarters and in the Home Office) according to unstated criteria and
unrevealed data. The existence of consultative committees has so far not made
local administrative decisions either much more participative or visible nor has
it been matched in most forces by any real devolution of resource allocation
powers to sub-divisional commanders.

That the police see no need or reason to disclose the basis on which their most
important managerial decisions are made is largely due to current
arrangements for the governance of the police. Because police authorities are
not constitutionally responsible for operational matters they behave
irresponsibly towards operational issues politically. Those committees and
members who are content with current policy, the majority, tend complacently
to ask few questions of the police: those who are critical of the police or
question them often dwell parochially on particular issues or incidents,
ostensibly defending the interests of particular groups or neighbourhoods but
assisting the police little with the resolution of the difficult overall policy
dilemmas they face. Both approaches symbiotically perpetuate the absence of
a well informed public debate on policing. The police generally collude with
this state of affairs. They allow those police authority members who uncritically
support them to bask in ignorance. On the other hand those members who
attempt to probe operational policy are assumed to have malevolent intentions,
are received defensively and are sometimes counter-attacked. Constructive
well informed dialogue is conspicuous by its absence.

The shortcomings of the police authorities are mirrored in the sub-divisional
consultative groups. Community groups hostile to the police generally boycott
committees on the grounds that they cannot determine operational policy. As a
result most committee members are supportive of the police but are inexpert,
ripe to absorb police accounts (including the need for increased resources) but
unable to determine whether current sevices are the best that can be provided
with available resources. To answer the question I posed at the beginning of this
paper, the citizens of Middleshire seldom discuss the operational policies which
affect them because they know insufficient about the services their
Constabulary provides and about the basis on which service delivery is
determined. The police reveal aspects of their organisation, but do so
superficially. They keep their operational cards close to their chests and do not
generally reveal their managerial problems: they regard the arena of local
politics, of which police consultative committees are becoming an integral part,
as dangerous terrain where they are liable to be attacked.

There is limited consultation about major police operations in some sub-divisions, but it is intermittent and partial. In the absence of a democratic framework for political accountability locally, the process typically generates a sequence of recrimination and counter-recrimination as to whether those who are consulted (usually appointed or self-selected persons) are representative of the community and whether they are watch-dogs or lap-dogs.

What of the future? Consultative committees are a recent innovation. In most areas they have existed only since 1983-84. It is too early to come to definitive conclusions about their impact. Participants are still learning the game, watching precedents and looking for good practices. It is possible that the police, prompted by Home Office circulars and the HM Inspectorate of Constabulary, will in future collect, analyse and disseminate more data about their activities and the demands made on them. It is possible that this educative process will generate a more constructive response, that a positive dialogue and genuine policy making partnership will be forged between the police, local politicians and representatives of other community groups. The early signs, however, do not inspire optimism. Within the existing constitutional framework a partnership is unlikely to develop unless the following nettles are grasped.

- *The fact that many police authorities and members seem not to take their duties seriously.* Members need to spend time and money educating themselves about the service for the efficiency and adequacy of which they are statutorily responsible. This means developing mechanisms capable of briefing members both nationally and locally. The Association of Metropolitan Police Authorities had begun this process before the Metropolitan Police Authorities were abolished; their pioneering efforts need emulating. If the government is serious about the concept of partnership, it may have to assist with this educative process.
- *The paucity of hard organisational and operational data provided to police authorities by chief constables.* Police authorities need to know the basis on which management decisions are taken and need to be consulted fully about the policy options available before irrevocable decisions are taken. Only then can issues meaningfully be put to consultative committees and grass roots opinion tapped. Consultative committees, at whatever level they operate, are unlikely to develop credibility unless members feel that what they have to say is important for the planning of police services.
- *The confusion and ignorance of consultative committee members.* If this is not remedied by the sort of top-down leadership implicit in the previous point, it could be reduced by bottom-up organisation and pressure. There is no reason why consultative committees should not periodically meet (possibly without the police being present) in order to consider what they exist for and to devise programmes and objectives. Nor is there any reason why they should not form an association to provide advice and devise guidelines for members. The primary task of consultative committees is to articulate the consumer's viewpoint and explore, with the police, the degree to which that viewpoint can be recognised in the way police services are delivered.

At various stages in this paper I have expressed doubts about the degree to which a substantive planning partnership between the police and the community is likely to develop. The idea may be wholly unrealistic: it is possible to argue that the very nature of policing - its contingent and combative character - is inimical to the whole notion of planning or partnership, not least because the impact of policing differentially affects the heterogeneous groups which make up any geographical community. Police officers are wont to argue for professional autonomy on precisely this basis. But it may be that the very possibility of partnership, however limited, is undermined by the current constitutional framework for the governance of the police. The absence of local politicians' formal responsibility for general operational policy (resource distribution, organisation, priorities, etc.) may lie at the root of their irresponsibility regarding policing. It is possible that the only way in which responsible discussion of policing will come about locally is by making politicians accountable for the fundamentally difficult decisions which at present the police tend, usually at their own insistence, to take alone behind largely closed doors.

Consultative committees, as presently constituted, are neither fish, nor fowl nor good red herring. First, they do not represent a community, however that term is defined: sub-divisions seldom coincide with self-identifying physical neighbourhoods or communities; they cut across them or span many. Second, with their limited memberships, the committees do not normally pretend to represent either the many 'interest communities' or neighbourhoods (Willmott, 1984) which make up sub-divisions. Third, committees seldom stress, even symbolically, political accountability: not only are they based on police administrative rather than local government areas, but their members are not directly elected. Committees normally comprise a mixture of councillors (self or pre-selected for this purpose), neighbourhood or interest group representatives, and officers from various statutory and voluntary agencies. It follows that, quite apart from their lack of power (which robs them of all credibility for some people), committees have no mandate or characteristic in common. As far as neighbourhoods are concerned they operate in the stratosphere. As far as professionals are concerned they are amateur. As far as politicians are concerned they are not representative or accountable.

Given that police policy is currently locally *administered*, the choice of the sub-division for consultation (outside London) is logical: by this method the line of police managerial accountability is clear. However, even without amendment to the constitutional arrangements for the governance of the police, there is reason to argue that partnership between the police and the local community will best be achieved if it is grafted on to local *government* systems of political accountability.

Interestingly, those few efforts being made to pursue inter-agency crime prevention initiatives as a result of Home Office Circular 8/1984 are generally being conducted at district council level and usually, our evidence suggests, without the involvement or knowledge of local politicians. There is a good case for forging links between these inter- agency initiatives and the framework for consultation.

Finally, whether consultation takes place on the basis of sub-divisional or district council boundaries, it is arguably at neighbourhood level (self-identifying communities of common interest) that there most needs to be consultation to articulate consumer concerns and mount practical initiatives. All the evidence suggests that people's fears of crime and anxieties about order are highly parochial. Whether committees need to be created for the purpose depends on the availability of existing networks. In many rural areas parish councils, visited when the need arises by local constables and occasionally more senior officers, are probably sufficient. But there is a need for an equivalent structure in urban areas (see Collingridge, 1986). Probably the most important task for sub-divisional or district council consultative committees is the monitoring of neighbourhood liaison arrangements, inquiring whether they are in place and working well. There could be no better starting point for penetrating much of the current rhetoric about community policing.

* * * * * *

The data on which this paper is based were collected as part of an ongoing research project on police community consultation processes funded by the Economic and Social Research Council and the Police Foundation. I am indebted to my colleagues in that research - Dr Christopher Maggs and Mr Paul Swift - for their assistance. Responsibility for the contents of this paper is, however, entirely my own.

References

Baldwin, R. and Kinsey, R. (1982) *Police Powers and Politics*, London, Quartet Books.

Bayley, D.H. (1983) 'Accountability and control of the police: some lessons for Britain' in T. Bennett (editor) *The Future of Policing*, Cambridge, Cropwood series, No 15.

Chief Constable of Merseyside (1986), *Annual Report for 1985*, Liverpool, Merseyside Constabulary.

Collingridge, J. (1986) 'The appeal of decentralisation', *Local Government Studies*, May-June.

Cox, G. (1986) 'Openness and accountability' in J. Benyon and C. Bourne (editors) *The Police: powers, procedures and proprieties*, London, Pergamon.

Downes, D. and Ward, J. (1986) *Democratic Policing: towards a Labour Party policy on policing*, London, Labour Campaign for Criminal Justice.

Fine, R. and Millar, R. (editors) (1985) *Policing the Miners' Strike*, London, Cobden Trust.

Home Office Circulars:

54/1982 *Local Consultation Arrangements between the Community and the Police*

114/1983 *Manpower, Effectiveness and Efficiency in the Police Service*

8/1984 *Crime Prevention*

2/1985 *Arrangements for Local Consultation between the Community and the Police Outside London*

12/1986 *Lay Visitors to Police Stations*.

Kinsey, R., Lea, J. and Young, J. (1986) *Losing the Fight Against Crime*, Oxford, Blackwell.

Kogan, M. (1986) *Education Accountability: an analytical overview*, London, Hutchinson.

Lord Scarman (1981) *Report of an Inquiry into the Brixton Disorder, 10-12 April 1981*, HMSO.

Lustgarten, L. (1986) *The Governance of the Police*, London, Sweet and Maxwell.

Morgan, R. and Maggs, C. (1985) *Setting the PACE: police community consultation arrangements in England and Wales*, Bath Social Policy Papers 4, Bath, University of Bath.

Morgan, R. (1986) 'Police consultative groups: the implications for the governance of the police', *Political Quarterly*, January-March.

Reiner, R. (1985) *The Politics of the Police*, London, Wheatsheaf.

Savage, S. (1984) 'Political control or community liaison?' *Political Quarterly*, Vol. 55, January-March.

Scraton, P. (1985) *The State of the Police*, London, Pluto.

Smith, B.J. (1985) *Decentralisation: the territorial dimension of the state*, London, Allen and Unwin.

Smith, D. (1986) 'The framework of law and policing practice' in J. Benyon and C. Bourne (editors) *The Police: powers, procedures and proprieties*, London, Pergamon.

Spencer, S. (1985) *Called to Account: the case for police accountability in England and Wales*, London, National Council of Civil Liberties.

Stewart, J., Deakin, N. and Wright, A. (1984) *Socialism and Decentralisation*, Fabian Tract 496, London, Fabian Society.

Waddington, P.A.J. (1986) 'Defining objectives: a response to Tony Butler', *Policing*, Spring.

Widdicombe Report (1986) *The Conduct of Local Authority Business: report of the Committee of Inquiry into the conduct of local authority business*, London, HMSO.

Willmott, P. (1984) *Community in Social Policy*, Discussion Paper 9, London, Policy Studies Institute.

5 COMMUNITY SAFETY, CRIME PREVENTION AND THE LOCAL AUTHORITY

Jon Bright

There has been unprecedented interest in crime prevention during the past 12 months. Until recently, it has always lagged a poor fourth in the criminal justice world, attracting much less attention than policing, juvenile offending and prisons. One reason for this new concern may be the realisation among politicians and the public that spending on the criminal justice system (probation, police, courts, penal establishments), up in real terms by 31 per cent since 1979, has had little or no impact on preventing crime or protecting people or reforming offenders. Crime rates have gone up, crime problems seriously concern a large proportion of the population, an extraordinarily high proportion of young offenders (70 to 80 per cent) reoffend on leaving youth custody or detention centres and England still continues to imprison more people at a younger age for longer periods than any other European country except Turkey.

A second reason for this growing interest in crime prevention may be the new information about crime and crime problems which a series of recent crime surveys have made available. In these surveys - two national (Hough and Mayhew, 1983; 1985) and two local (Kinsey, 1984; Jones, Maclean and Young, 1986) - attempts have been made to assess the extent of crime by interviewing people about their experiences as victims. These surveys suggest that, overall, there is about four times as much crime as is reported to and recorded by the police, and a very much higher figure for crimes such as sexual assault and criminal damage.

The two national crime surveys demonstrate that, despite what amounts to a massive under-reporting of crime, most crime is relatively minor: 80 per cent involves theft, handling and burglary; 30 per cent involves motor vehicles; over half of all offences and three-quarters of burglaries are committed by people under 21; most burglary losses are less than £50 and the *average* chances of being a victim are slight (for burglary, once in every 40 years and for robbery, once in every 500 years). The main significance of the British Crime Survey is that it has suggested that much crime, reported or recorded or not, may be prevented.

However, an even more important stimulus to crime prevention has come from the 1984 national survey and the two local ones. These have drawn attention to the uneven distribution of crime within the population. For example, it has become clear that burglary, vandalism, sexual assault, robbery and other crimes of violence, the types of crime with which the public are most concerned, disproportionately affect people on low incomes, those living in inner urban areas, some ethnic minority groups and young women. Crime is geographically concentrated and its impact focussed on specific population groups. Aggregate victim surveys are almost as misleading as official crime statistics. The average likelihood quoted above of being a victim of crime should be contrasted with the one in four likelihood of burglary for residents living in high risk inner city areas and one in five for those living on the poorest council estates. Besides masking the geographical concentration of crime, aggregate figures are also insensitive to domestic violence and sexual assault.

A third reason for the new interest in preventing crime is the growing knowledge about fear of crime, its causes and consequences. It is necessary to distinguish between fear of crime on the one hand and a concern about crime that leads people to take sensible precautions but does not significantly constrain their life style. Fear is a serious social problem even in areas where crime levels are relatively low. Women are particularly affected. The anxiety may be linked to reports of high crime rates in depressed urban areas that are then assumed to apply locally, and the way in which the media, particularly local newspapers, are prone to exaggerate and sensationalise crime. Because of the higher levels of crime in the more disadvantaged areas, there is also greater fear of crime there. This has been exacerbated by large scale redevelopment since the 1950s, particularly when it resulted in physical forms that attract anti-social and criminal behaviour and discouraged the growth of neighbourliness.

All crime surveys indicate that fear of crime is a more serious problem in areas where the real risks of being a victim are higher and it is also associated with a generalised dissatisfaction with particular neighbourhoods. It is therefore a serious phenomenon in its own right. It can lead to social segregation; those who can move away do so. It causes those who remain to retreat into their homes. The 'public sphere' is thereby undermined, leading to a reduction in the informal community controls that can contain anti-social and petty criminal behaviour. And some residents become stressed, anxious and obsessive. This sort of scenario is typical of many inner ciy and outer urban areas. It demands a response based on organised resources necessary to maintain an adequate level of services and facilities. If the infrastructure of a neighbourhood is allowed to decay, we should not be surprised if there is an increase in the crime rate or that many people fear crime or that parents do not know how to prevent their children becoming offenders. But perhaps the most significant factor in the increased interest in crime prevention is the political attention it attracts. Crime prevention has become an issue with which opposition parties have challenged the government's claim to be the guardian of law and order. Indeed, the Labour Party made crime prevention one of the major themes of its recently published policy document *Fairness and Freedom* (1986) along with housing, health, transport and education.

It would be wrong to criticise the government for doing nothing about crime prevention. However, it has been highly selective in the use it has made of the interdepartmental circular (Home Office, 8/1984) as a basis for crime prevention policy. Costs have been kept low, neighbourhood watch schemes have proliferated but the mounting problems of crime in run down areas are hardly being considered. Indeed, government crime prevention policy might be said to represent a mixture of public relations exercises containing much rhetoric but little substance, combined with initiatives and projects of varying ingenuity but minimal expenditure. The measures proposed so far by the government have very little to offer the people living in the areas where crime problems are most severe.

It is now necessary to tease out from all the rhetoric what actually needs to be done, who should do it, who should manage it, how it should be paid for and what should be the role of the community itself in the process.

The police

There has until recently been a generally accepted assumption that the police are the agency with principal responsibility for preventing crime. The police themselves acknowledge a tendency on their part 'to corner the market in crime prevention and detection and to assume that they were the sole agency with responsibility for community order' (Newman, 1983). No other agency seemed particularly concerned to challenge this monopoly. All this has now changed. Increased spending on the police has done nothing to halt the rising level of crime or impove the clear up rates. At the same time there has been increasing criticism of a number of police forces directed at their ineffectiveness, lack of accountability and their repeated failure to deal adequately with cases of serious misconduct in their own ranks. These criticisms are made not only by Labour councils and police monitoring groups; Bernard Levin made the points powerfully in a *Times* article (1985), and there is a great deal of unpublicised concern in some government circles.

Indeed, a series of Home Office research papers have pointed to the limitations of police action in preventing crime and the circular on crime prevention (Home Office Circular 8/1984) was intended to reappraise the balance of responsibilities for crime control between the police, the local authorities and local communities. However, this new approach offered no extra cash; local authorities were simply exhorted to do more with less. The police were now expected to work much more closely with statutory and voluntary agencies and with local communities. The so-called co-ordinated approach to controlling crime has become accepted wisdom, although it is a measure of the degree of professional isolation of the police that this common sense idea should be thought so novel. The view that now prevails therefore is that the police cannot control crime on their own. A co-ordinated multi-agency approach is required in order to establish the formal 'management' controls in residential areas that are a precondition for the development of the sorts of informal community controls that might be expected to deter anti-social or petty criminal behaviour.

This view is plausible but inevitably leads on to the issues of police accountability, efficiency, priorities and the status of the police in inter-agency collaboration. Interestingly, the Islington Crime Survey contests elements of this 'new' approach (Jones, Maclean and Young, 1986). It argues that not only are police priorities not in accord with those of the people they police but that there is room for considerable improvement in police effectiveness at controlling the crimes that most concern the majority of people - street robbery with violence, sexual assault, use of hard drugs, residential burglary, drunken driving and racist attacks - and this is where police efforts should be directed.

The Islington survey does not accept that, because much crime is opportunistic, it is therefore unpreventable or that the service role and order maintenance role of the police should be expanded, as the Metropolitan Police proposes to do. The survey implies that there are clear limits to the type and number of crimes that can be prevented or deterred by inter-agency cooperation or informal community controls and that the police should recognise this. Also part of the reason for poor police performance is the very low level of public cooperation that exists in many urban areas. Crime control is dependent on good police/public relations - 95 per cent of all crimes come to the attention of the police from the public - but there is a significant proportion of people from a number of social groups who distrust the police and will not cooperate at any stage of the judicial process. Unless this issue is addressed, a significant improvement in performance is unlikely.

The Islington suvey report argues that 'crime control should be public-initiated and reactive rather than police-initiated and proactive, their service role transferred to other agencies and police tasks rationalised in order to maximise productivity in terms of crime control'. However, this view appears to be slightly at odds with various neighbourhood policing strategies which are seemingly a response to community demands for visible policing and which form part of a number of experimental improvement schemes throughout the country, a few of which are demonstrably successful at reducing crime.

In connection with the contribution of policing to crime prevention and the relationship of the police to the community at a local level, the Safe Neighbourhoods Unit working in London has found, with a few important exceptions, that

- on many estates, people have unrealistic expectations of neighbourhood policing;
- home beats are generally far too large;
- police officers do not make productive contact with the community;
- police officers do not plan their policing with the community's representatives;
- there appears to be no method or system to neighbourhood policing;
- home beat officers are not attached to one beat for very long;
- there is an overemphasis on neighbourhood watch;
- there is a lack of confidence and trust in the police by significant sections of the black community;
- many people believe there is no effective way of preventing abuse of authority by police officers;
- there is no effective grievance procedure for aggrieved members of the community; and
- there is an emphasis on liaison, PR and attendance at meetings, but little corresponding change ('on the ground').

NACRO's experiences in areas outside London were very varied. It is clear that some police forces have been making great efforts to develop their community role (for example, West Midlands and South Wales) while some others have not. In general the following points could be made:
- a change in officers (at all levels) could have a dramatic effect on the nature of policing in an area; continuity of policy was at the mercy of staff changes;
- not enough attention seemed to be paid to developing job descriptions for home beat/permanent beat officers;
- the role of the home beat officer was undervalued and beat officers were often withdrawn from beat duties to perform 'more important duties' (for example crowd control);
- where police officers were making substantial community inputs (for example helping to develop youth clubs), not enough attention was given to helping community groups to run their own affairs so that, when the police inputs were reduced or withdrawn, initiatives did not collapse.

Detailed recommendations addressing these issues can be found in the Unit's reports (for example, Safe Neighbourhoods Unit, forthcoming) and in the NACRO Crime Prevention Advisory Committee Working Group report on policing council estates (NACRO, forthcoming).

The role of the local authority
The term 'community safety' is now commonly used in order to broaden the concept of crime prevention from its rather narrow associations with the police, security technology and control in order to encompass the wider issues of protection and the role of the local authority in the creation of safe environments. We would advocate an expansion of the local government role in this area and the development of local community safety strategies within a framework of localised service provision, corporate management, inter-agency cooperation and resident participation.

A framework for a community safety policy might look like this (these ideas are developed further in a Safe Neighbourhoods Unit forthcoming publication *Confronting Crime: Community Safety and Crime Prevention*):

Strategies to reduce crime: Council structures and procedures:
- promotion of good neighbourhood management;
- reports to committees;
- establishment of community safety committees and units;
- establishment of an emergency safety fund;
- raising staff awareness and increasing skills;
- development of information systems: crime mapping, crime surveys, crime audits;
- raising public awareness.

Protecting groups most at risk:
- preventing crime against women;
- preventing crime against ethnic groups;

-   preventing crime against children.

Implementing community safety/crime prevention measures:
-   in owner occupied/private rented residential areas;
-   on local authority housing estates;
-   on public transport.

Community responses to offending:
-   promotion of minimum standards of youth and play provision;
-   development of locally basd employment opportunities;
-   engagement with the criminal justice system.

Services for victims of crime:
-   the need for victim services; - victim support schemes;
-   criminal injuries compensation.

Policing local authority housing estates:
-   authority/police cooperation (at authority level);
-   home beat policing strategies;
-   strategies for resident participation (estate or area level).

To a large extent, public expectations of policing are unrealistic and come about because of a failure to resource other networks of control and order. In the case of council housing estates, it cannot be stressed too strongly that the security and safety of tenants depends to a large extent on the local authority's ability to improve, manage and maintain its estates and to ensure, for example, that they are provided with adequate youth and community facilities. A major investment in public sector housing is required to enable councils to do this, yet since 1979 there has been a 60 per cent cut in Housing Investment Programme allocations (the amount of money local authorities are allowed to borrow to invest in council housing) as well as restrictive legislation and numerous other financial controls. For every pound spent in 1979, local authorities are now only able to spend 26p. In addition, the Audit Commission's report on housing management (1986) concluded that the government must respond to the estimated £19 billion council housing disrepair bill if local authorities are to improve services to their tenants.

These controls need to be relaxed and the determination of local government expenditure more closely related to the task of regenerating depressed urban areas. If this were done, local authorities would be required to ensure that all council properties were fitted with effective door and window security and that additional arrangements were made to enhance the safety and security of tenants living in multi-storey blocks, on high density flatted estates and in areas where crime problems are known to exist. Housing management and repairs services need to be localised and made considerably more responsive and accountable to tenants than they are in many areas at present. It is not just a question of resources; political will, imagination and flexibility are required if councils are to become better landlords and to be able to confront the bureaucratic inertia that limits the effectiveness of so many of them.

Tenants on many flatted estates think that their security would be enhanced by the employment of resident caretakers with clear responsibility for the upkeep of particular blocks; they feel that receptionists or door porters should be located in glass-fronted offices in the entrance lobbies of multi-storey blocks from which they could directly control access. There has been a tendency to exaggerate the effectiveness of physical security measures in such blocks. Evidence strongly suggests that it is a human presence which deters burglars, who appear to avoid the risk of confrontation; unmanned alternatives to door porters in multi-storey blocks, such as phone entry systems, are far less effective.

It is important also that the implementation of such measures is planned in accordance wth the wishes of the local community. The success of crime prevention strategies, particularly on public housing estates, will often depend on the extent to which residents have participated in formulating them.

The responsibility of the local authority in this area is not confined to meeting its obligations to its tenants. Resources are also required for developing adequate play and youth facilities. These are vitally important in their own right and there are obvious links between, on the one hand, society's failure to provide for the social and recreational needs of children and young people and levels of vandalism and juvenile offending. Councils need to give more support to tenants' and residents' organisations to enable communities to articulate their needs and participate in planning the improvement of their neighbourhoods. In fact, in the case of council tenants, local authorities should be empowered and required to provide properly constituted tenants' organisations with an independent and reliable source of funding on a capitation basis. Real community development and tenant participation in housing management is meaningless without this.

There should also be a duty upon local authorities to conduct regular surveys of local crime problems and to coordinate the response of their own departments, the police, tenants and residents groups, commercial interests and voluntary bodies. Given the under-recording of crime by the police, local surveys are the only way in which crime problems can be reliably assessed. Low cost insurance schemes administered by local authorities should be provided for council tenants and low income groups and a national scheme set up to provide crime prevention advice and grants for door and window locks and other security devices. There should be increased investment in equipment and staffing on public transport, to improve the safety of users and workers alike, and financial support is required for local schemes to help victims of crime (such as Rape Crisis Centres, Women's Refuges and Victim Support Schemes).

Conclusion

A new approach to crime prevention and community safety means clarifying the respective roles of the police and other public agencies. There is a dimension to the problem of crime control (the detection and apprehension of offenders) that only the police can deal with, but the main preventive role should fall on local authorities, in cooperation with the police, other relevant organisations and local communities. The financial implications of this extension of local government need to be recognised. We must look closely at the way neighbourhoods are managed and serviced and at the nature of the community's input into this process and control over it. We must realise that a proper level of investment in buildings, services and facilities in run-down areas is essential if any impact is to be made on crime problems. This is particularly urgent given the massive disinvestment of resources during the past six years from the areas where crime problems are most acute and the abolition of the GLC and the Metropolitan County Councils, which had begun to make real efforts to address these issues.

This paper is not advocating uncontrolled public expenditure. Its central argument is that crime problems have been exacerbated by the withdrawal of resources from the depressed parts of our cities and that a reduction in crime might be expected to follow a return to levels of investment sufficient to sustain viable neighbourhoods. Crime itself imposes an increasingly heavy financial burden on society through expenditure on the criminal justice system (£4,800 million on prisons, police, courts and probation service in 1986-87) as well as the costs to local authorities and the victims themselves (Her Majesty's Treasury, 1986). A broadly-based, well thought out, preventive strategy is not only likely to be more effective in reducing crime problems but makes good financial sense as well. A criminal justice policy must be devised which moves away from an almost exclusive concern with public order maintenance and processing offenders to one which lays equal emphasis on protection and prevention and on the humane treatment and rehabilitation of offenders.

* * * * * *

Jon Bright is Co-ordinator of the Safe Neighbourhoods Unit, a project set up by NACRO to assist with the improvement of conditions on London housing estates. This article, an earlier version of which was published in *Crime and Social Justice*, the Prison Reform Trust and Christian Action journal, Autumn 1986, constitutes a personal viewpoint. Acknowledgements to David Birley and Paul Cavadino for their comments on an early draft.

References
Audit Commission (1986) *Managing the Crisis in Council Housing*, London, HMSO.
Her Majesty's Treasury (1986) *The Government's Expenditure Plans 1986-87 to 1988-89*, Cmnd 9702, I and II, London, HMSO.
Home Office Circular 8/1984 *Crime Prevention*.
Hough, M. and Mayhew, P. (1983) *The British Crime Survey: first report*, Home Office Research Study 76, London, HMSO.
Hough, M. and Mayhew, P. (1985) *Taking Account of Crime: key findings from the second British Crime Survey*, Home Office Research Study 85, London, HMSO.
Jones, T., Maclean, B. and Young, J. (1986) *The Islington Crime Survey: crime, victimisation and policing in inner-city London*, Aldershot, Gower.
Kinsey, R. (1984) *Merseyside Crime Survey: first report*, Liverpool, Police

Committee Support Unit.

Labour Party (1986) *Freedom and Fairness Campaign: putting people first*, a campaign pack, London, Labour Party.

Levin, B. (1985) 'Who will defend us against the boys in blue?', *The Times*, 17 December 1985.

NACRO (forthcoming) Crime Prevention Advisory Committee Working Group, *Policing Council Housing Estates*, London, NACRO.

Newman, K. (1984) *Report of the Commissioner of Police for the Metropolis 1983*, London, HMSO.

Safe Neighbourhoods Unit (forthcoming) *Confronting Crime: community safety and crime prevention*, London, SNU.

6 THE POLICE AND THE IDEA OF COMMUNITY
David Smith

This seminar is part of a programme of research and discussion on the idea of comunity and its deployment in many areas of social policy. The wider framework is important. Our subject is not just the particular initiatives and proposals that have been marketed under the 'community policing' brand name (a name like 'Spar' that gives a common identity to a diverse range of independent concerns). More broadly, our subject is the use of the idea of community in thinking about policing and the links between its application in that field and increasingly in every other field of policy.

The idea of community
To establish this wider framework, it is useful to go back to the analysis provided by Peter Willmott in *Community in Social Policy (1984)*. He writes that the word can be used in one of three ways. It can mean the *territorial community* where what people have in common is residence in a particular geographical area, normally a fairly small locality, but sometimes the whole country, in which case the community is used to mean just everybody; or it can refer to the *community of interest*, based on occupation, ethnic group, leisure pursuits, sexual orientation, and so on; or it can mean the more elusive *community of attachment*, with a community sense or spirit built on social interaction and a sense of identity.

He lists a number of recent and current social changes that have tended to erode community sense: increasing residential mobility, housing clearance schemes, increasing remoteness of institutions, changes in retailing patterns (longer journeys to large shopping centres), increasing personal mobility (for some but not all), home-centred entertainment. But he also notes some developments that may be expected to increase community sense: more time is likely to be spent in the locality because of high unemployment, because retirement ages are lower and because the old form an increasing proportion of the population; there may in future be less travel because of financial and energy constraints; economic developments like wordprocessing may cause more people to work at home. Community sense was probably never as strong as some people like to pretend. There are some areas where it is conspicuously absent, and this lack is associated with a whole range of social problems. Yet, after taking account of the trends and counter trends, community sense and the associated local or small-scale institutions will persist, and they represent a resource that social policy can make use of.

Willmott goes on in his paper to describe a wide range of applications of the idea of community in social policy. These include community work (helping a local community to deal with a problem such as high crime on a council estate); community organisations (of a federal or umbrella type); community groups (with specific objects, such as a play association, women's aid or a tenants' association); community arts; community media (local radio, cable television, but apparently not local newspapers); community care (providing medical and social care in the locality and incorporating them with the informal care that people give each other); community social work (which again makes use of informal networks of care); local government decentralisation; community education (using schools for the benefit of the whole of the local community); and, of course, community policing.

Among these various applications of the idea of community, he detects a range of objectives: the delivery of local services; linking formal with informal care; the devolution of power and the development of consultation; improvements in the local environment and in the local collective welfare; helping people develop their capacities; development of a more pluralistic society (with a choice of 'alternatives' to mainstream theatre, housing, diet and so on); development of political education; and development of community sense. This is to describe the objectives at a fairly detailed level. Taking a broader view, a common theme underlying all of the initiatives is a reaction against large scale and remoteness ('small is beautiful'). And there are two very general aims: to help people come together in meeting their needs and tackling common problems; and to encourage public policy and practice to strengthen voluntary and informal structures and work with rather than against them.

Willmott recognises that different groups have conflicting interests but he assumes that the right course is to seek a resolution to these conflicts through bargaining. He does not particularly emphasise or further explore this problem, which assumes great importance when we come to consider policing. He gives greater emphasis to a number of other difficulties. Participation in the local community is bound to play a small part in the lives of most people. It can do nothing about poverty (as the history of the community development programme has shown). Either participation means consultation but without devolving power and influence, in which case it means little; or if it does mean devolving power it must lead to confusion, inaction, delays and cynicism. There is no available test to show whether community spokesmen are representative. There are doubts about the effectiveness of particular projects in practice and there has been little, if any, scientific evaluation of what they have achieved.

Application of the idea of community to policing
Belief in something called community policing has become the current orthodoxy in English-speaking countries. This is vividly expressed in the opening address at a conference organised by the Australian Institute of Criminology in 1984. The speaker is Mr P.T. Anderson, the Minister of Police and Emergency Services in New South Wales.

I think it can be safely said that a vast majority of the world's most progressive police forces have implemented community policing in one form or another and it is the topic on the lips of those police forces in the world at the present time who have come to the realisation that 'traditional' policing methods are not enough.

Last year I had the privilege of undertaking a study tour which included amongst many aspects of policing an examination of community policing practices and procedures and community relations bureaux in operation in a number of major centres throughout the world. These included Washington, London and Hong Kong.

It would be an understatement to say that I was more than impressed by the activities and programs implemented by these police forces.

The term community policing sometimes describes a total approach, but sometimes refers to just one element in the pattern of policing or just one unit within the organisation (such as the permanent beat officer); the term can also be attached to particular, sometimes local, initiatives that are meant to mesh with the community in some way. These initiatives and approaches can be fairly diverse, but the use of the term is broadly speaking understandable and it does fit in with Willmott's analysis of the idea of community in its various applications. Without making any statement about what community policing delivers in practice, the broad themes that Willmott identifies do underlie virtually all conceptions of what it is *meant* to be. It *is* a reaction against large scale and remoteness (and, one might add, impersonality). This is most clearly expressed in the idea of the community beat officer who is meant to have a continuous relationship with a small area (or 'local community'); this idea of course co-exists with the idea of fire-brigade policing by officers in fast cars who cover a much wider area, but is also a reaction against it.

Again, most conceptions of community policing *do* promise to help people come together in meeting their needs and tackling common problems. In the context of policing, this is called the multi-agency approach to the prevention of crime and public disorder, with the police acting as leaders or catalysts. Further, an important objective of community policing approaches *is* to strengthen voluntary and informal structures of social control and crime prevention and to work with rather than against them (the paper by Joanna Shapland and Jon Vagg sees this objective as the central one).

Community policing is also linked with the development of consultation. This raises, as in the case of these other initiatives, the difficulty that consultation on its own does not amount to much, but substantive devolution of power would conflict with other objectives. Some of the other problems that are mentioned as hindering the application of the idea of community do arise in the case of community policing in particular. In general, people participate in the local community to only a limited extent and are bound to do so; in specific terms, not many people want to come to meetings to talk about policing and crime prevention, and in some areas most people will not participate in neighbourhood watch schemes. It has been shown that community activity can do nothing about poverty; perhaps it can also do little to counteract a downward spiral of disorganisation and demoralisation in poor and deprived areas. There is a general worry about whether community spokesmen are representative: this arises in a more acute and specific form when they are talking about the police. There is a general question about the effectiveness of community projects in practice, which restates itself with increasing urgency, as Mollie Weatheritt shows in her paper, when community policing projects are considered. Finally, there is not much scientific evaluation of community projects in general, and equally little of community policing projects in particular.

In all of these ways, then, community policing is a particular application of more general ideas about community and social policy that have become increasingly influential in recent years. The strength and appeal of the underlying ideas is much the same in this particular application as in the others; and the limitations and problems that arise in other fields of social policy can also arise in the case of policing - in fact, they may express themselves in a particularly acute form.

The theory of community policing
Three broad themes have been identified in thinking about the idea of community in social policy. First, there is the reaction against large scale and remoteness; this is associated with a demand for decentralisation and for consultation and participation in decision making by local communities. Second, there is the suggestion that people should come together to meet their common needs and to tackle common problems. Third, it is said that public policy and practice should act to strengthen voluntary and informal structures and work with and not against them. In the field of policing policy and practice, these ideas have expressed themselves in various ways.

Perhaps the most important is a renewed emphasis on permanent beat officers as a central element of policing. What is distinctive about them is that (when not withdrawn and assigned to other duties) they work continuously within very small areas: the beats in Portsmouth, for example, have a population of about 12,000. This is in contrast to the officers on uniform reliefs, who generally patrol in vehicles over a whole sub-division (a population of 60,000 to 100,000) or patrol on foot in different areas from one day to the next; and in still greater contrast to the officers in specialist units, who generally cover much larger areas such as a division or the territory of the whole force. In detail there may be many different views about what permanent beat officers should do and how they should do it, but it is common ground that they should get to know people and be known, that they should be seen out and about and that they should make contact with or participate in local groups and organisations. An increased emphasis on permanent beat officers also implies a shift in the balance towards foot patrol (except in rural areas, where these officers may go about on motor cycles).

The second feature of community policing is an emphasis on prevention rather than apprehension. In principle, it is possible to imagine comprehensive programmes for the prevention of crime and public disorder. They would start by systematically collecting and analysing information about specific kinds of crime and disorder (and about all demands on the police) at a local level. Next, strategies for preventing some specific kinds of crime and disorder would be developed by the police in partnership with voluntary and other official agencies. Then, through the various agencies, the police would mobilise the whole community to implement these strategies. In practice, crime prevention initiatives have been much more modest, and many of them have been carried out by the police acting largely on their own; but the idea of coordinated crime prevention strategies is emphasised in the context of community policing.

A third application of the idea of community to policing is the multi-agency approach. This is the suggestion that the police should work in partnership with other agencies, voluntary and official. It is implicit in the coordinated approach to crime prevention, but it may also be used to pursue other objectives, for example helping the victims of crime or dealing with mental illness.

A fourth element in community policing ideas is consultation combined with decentralisation and the devolution of power. The one concrete change in this area has been the creation of the police consultative groups, though there have also been some attempts (notably in the Metropolitan Police) to devolve decision making to the level at which the consultation takes place. Closely related to consultation is openness and the sharing of information. As evidence that the police are, in fact, becoming more open, far more researchers have gained access to police forces in the past 10 years than previously. The scheme for allowing access of lay visitors to police stations is also a significant development.

A fifth element is a greater emphasis on activity initiated by the police rather than response to calls from the public. This emphasis relates more closely to the idea of rational planning than to the idea of community. The argument is that the police should study the problems they have to deal with in a measured way, then formulate plans for dealing with them; this will mean defining tasks, deciding priorities and allocating resources so as to deal with the problems most effectively. To be able to do this, the police must prevent their resources from being used entirely in responding to immediate demands by the public, and instead direct some of them to police-initiated activities. This approach is often linked with community policing ideas because it is assumed that the problems (and possibly the solutions) will be defined in consultation with local groups and voluntary organisations at the local level and other official bodies. At a less analytical level, the customary rhetoric equates 'fire brigade policing' with an impersonal, large scale and non-consultative approach, and 'proactive policing' with a concern for local communities. Finally, those who talk about community policing tend to emphasise the importance of informal social controls; they stress the responsibility of the community as a whole for the prevention of crime and disorder (as Mollie Weatheritt points out, this has been the central plank of official propaganda for 20 years or more); they point out that the police can do little or nothing on their own and that they need the support and help of the community; and by stressing common interests and objectives and playing down tensions and conflicts they try to talk up confidence in the police.

The practice of community policing

There is now accumulating evidence that in practice the application of the idea of community to policing has either made little difference or has not produced the intended results. What I mainly want to consider is the reasons for this failure and the prospects for future success. This is not the place to document the evidence about present and past initiatives, especially since other contributors have covered much of this ground. But it is worth giving some illustrations of ways in which results have been disappointing before going on to consider why.

The clearest example of the application of the idea of community in policing is probably the renewed emphasis on permanent beat officers. There is little indication that this has had a significant effect on the pattern or nature of policing. Perhaps the most important point is that, despite the impression that is sometimes created in public discussion, permanent beat officers are only a small proportion of the manpower in all forces, typically about 5 per cent. Policing is basically carried out by uniform reliefs and specialist units, while permanent beat officers are a small additional resource. Even in Hampshire, where there has been a substantial transfer of manpower to permanent beats, they still account for only 15 per cent of officers up to the rank of inspector. In other forces, permanent beat officers are certainly not the bread and butter of policing; they are just a bit of icing on the cake.

An interesting study of the work of permanent beat officers (they called them community constables) was carried out by the Home Office Research and Planning Unit in 1981-82 (Brown and Iles, 1985). The research covered a diverse set of sub-divisions, both urban and rural, in five police forces. The researchers provide a breakdown of the time spent by permanent beat officers on various activities, from diaries they were asked to fill in for a sample period. The bulk of their time was spent on 'general duties' (such as paperwork, court, refreshments) and withdrawn from their beats to meet other requirements (such as public order duties). Nearly a quarter of their time was spent patrolling on foot, but this involved hardly any interaction with local people. Just 14 per cent of their time was spent in community involvement and 10 per cent was spent on crime work, mostly carrying out investigations in relation to very minor matters, often for other forces. On average, the community involvement work amounted to five hours a week. Three of these hours were spent in informal contacts and rather less than one hour each on schools liaison and involvement with clubs and community groups. One-tenth of an hour a week was spent in liaison with statutory agencies. So much for the multi-agency approach.

Thus, in late 1981, there was no indication that permanent beat officers were, in general, engaging with the community to any significant extent. Of course, it might have been happening somewhere, for example in Hampshire - we all have to make exceptions of the forces where we are doing our own research - but in general, permanent beat officers were a fairly small group with marginal significance and whose tasks had not been clearly defined. Naturally, we will be told that now everything has changed. Perhaps Peter Willmott can now book a room for a seminar in 1988 to review the evidence on that point.

An important consequence of the application of the idea of community to policing has been a renewed emphasis on foot patrol. Police in vehicles answering calls over a wide area have been equated with large scale and centralisation, while officers on foot (or perhaps on a wobbly bicycle) have been equated with the capacity to engage with the community and respond to its needs. But there is very little evidence to show that a shift in the balance towards foot patrol is a successful policy. It is true that the Network foot patrol experiment (Police Foundation, Washington, 1981) appeared to demonstrate a decline in the fear of crime associated with an increase in the level of foot patrols, but it could not show any more tangible benefit. Th results of British initiatives, which have been critically appraised in *Innovations in Policing* (Weatheritt, 1985) are still less encouraging. Much the most thoroughly researched initiative was the one in Chelmsey Wood in 1983. Over the period of the experiment there was an increase in the level of foot patrol combined with a number of other apparently progressive changes. There was no increase among police officers in their knowledge of local people or problems or local crime patterns; reported crime rose; there was no improvement in the visibility of the police to local people and no decrease in the fear of crime.

A third illustration is the coordinated approach to crime prevention, an approach that gives central importance to developing links between the police and other agencies, voluntary and official. The weightiest initiative of this kind was the Home Office demonstration project in Greater Manchester, which had the objective of preventing school burglaries. The evaluation by the Home Office Research and Planning Unit (Hope, 1985) concludes that the initiative was not a success, largely because of problems of implementation; the preventive measures were mostly not taken, since those responsible had other preoccupations. According to the Home Office's analysis of its own project, the multi-agency approach was the main reason for failure. Because a number of agencies were involved, none of them had sole or prime responsibility, and none had to give the matter the highest priority. However, it is not just the coordinated crime prevention projects that have been disappointing. There is not much evidence, either, of success for more limited projects by the police working on their own (Weatheritt, 1985).

A fourth illustration is the police consultative groups, which are a clear response to the demand that the police should mesh with local communities. At present Rod Morgan can give us only the preliminary results from his research, but I am rash enough to predict that the following broad conclusions will be confirmed.

Because they do not have enough information or professional advice, the consultative groups are not able to engage in an intelligent discussion on equal terms with local police managers about policing policy and practice. As a result, the discussion tends to be ritualistic. Once a group has got through the early stages (in which there will be a fair amount of anti-police posturing in left-wing areas) it will generally become a means whereby the police confer legitimacy on the policies and practices they have decided to adopt. To say that the groups are used to confer legitimacy is, of course, different from saying (as the hard left do) that they are used to impose direct control on the community or that through them the community is successfully coopted to participate actively in pursuing police-defined objectives. (For the perspective from the left see, for example, Gordon, 1984.)

The underlying problems
It is not too difficult to see that problems of a fundamental nature arise when the idea of community is applied to policing, and that these underlying problems account for the poor results from the community policing approach. In fact, the use of the term 'community policing' is often a way of ducking the difficult questions that inevitably intervene as we struggle towards formulating coherent policing policies: for example, the question of how to achieve a balance between the wishes of the community and the rule of the law. It may be that some of the same problems underlie the use of the idea of community in other fields of social policy, too. It would be helpful to distinguish the common, and therefore general, problems from those that come up in a particular context or application.

Although the idea of community policing, if it is taken seriously (which it usually is not), begs just about every question that can be raised about policing, I will confine myself to mentioning five underlying problems.
- Police-initiated activity is mostly adversarial: consensus-building activity is hard to plan.
- Policing impinges on different sections of the community in contrasting ways.
- Decentralisation conflicts with the universal framework of law.
- Formal controls contrast with informal ones, and informal controls are hard to control formally.
- The idea of community cannot help with the distribution of resources.
In the rest of this paper I develop each of these points.

Planning for consensus
Most purposeful police work (this excludes patrolling as such) is directly initiated by demands from individual members of the public. This can best be demonstrated from facts about encounters between people and police officers. A number of studies have shown that most of these encounters are initiated by members of the public (Reiss, 1971; Kelling et al., 1980; Smith, 1983; Southgate and Ekblom, 1984). This means that, to a large extent, the pattern of policing is a response to consumer demand and not the result of a conscious plan. It can be argued that the pattern of demand is partly a response to the nature of the service provided in the past; this is to say that the police create the demand for their services rather as a manufacturer creates a demand for his product (Smith, 1983). But this still leaves little scope for direct control of the pattern of policing. This fundamental limitation makes all rational planning of police work difficult, except for planning to provide the resources to meet the pattern of demand as it presents itself.

Studies of police/public encounters are also united in showing that contacts initiated by the police are nearly all adversarial, whereas the great majority of contacts initiated by the public involve the delivery of a service. The clearest evidence on this point is from the British Crime Survey (Southgate and Ekblom, 1984).

Advocates of community policing assume that in consultation with local communities the police can plan and execute a programme of consensus-building activities. However, most consensus-building activity by the police occurs when they are providing a service in direct response to immediate demands by individual members of the public; it cannot, therefore, be easily planned. The activities that the police can readily plan, because they themselves initiate them, are mostly adversarial.

This is, of course, one of the major reasons why consultative groups tend to be used to legitimise plans (such as a drive against street robberies) that are likely to sharpen conflict with certain groups. They are not used to legitimise consensus-building plans because there are no consensus-building plans for them to legitimise. Also, when the police are providing a service by responding to immediate demands from members of the public, there is comparatively little need for discussion and negotiation about what they do; the pattern of their activity is governed by the market and to a large extent the market is an expression of the community's views. There *is* a need for discussion and negotiation about the pattern of police-initiated and adversarial activity but, as I argue below in discussing consensus and conflict, the idea of community does not provide us with a model that helps to resolve the acute conflicts that are likely to arise about this kind of policing.

The result, in practical terms, is the one that we have seen. Community policing means increasing the level of foot patrol without any real purpose (this *is* a consensus-building plan, but only in the sense that people tend to be in favour of it without knowing whether or not it achieves anything in concrete terms); and having some police officers make some positive contacts of a rather stereotyped and limited kind (for example, school visits). It may also mean trying to devise crime prevention projects, but these are also very difficult to plan and manage, especially if other agencies are involved, and they probably require a substantial input of extra resources if they are to achieve results (see Jon Bright's paper).

Another way of putting this is to say that the problem is to write a job description for community police officers that would concentrate on self-initiated activity and define a set of specific and concrete tasks. It may not be impossible to do that, but it has not been done yet. Perhaps it would be easier to envisage a real role for community police officers if they were the pivot of properly resourced crime prevention programmes. Again, nothing of that kind has happened so far. There have, of course, been crime prevention officers in all police forces since the late 1960s, but they do not have a close relationship with the mainstream of policing; in spite of the recommendations of an Association of Chief Police Offices working party in 1979, they carry out a narrow range of tasks; they do not adopt community-based approaches to crime prevention, and the extra resources that would be required to make these approaches work are not available (Weatheritt, 1985).

Conflict and consensus: the difficult publics

The word community is used to mean at least three different things: just everybody (or a number of fellow-residents), an interest group or a 'community of attachment'. But this clarification conceals the particular attraction of the idea: the way it encourages skilful jumps from one of these levels to another. The idea of community policing suggests (because of the 'just everybody' meaning of community) that there is a consensus about the kind of policing that is wanted. But in reality, policing is about dealing with conflict. Only in a centralised, authoritarian state would there be consensus about it.

Policing affects different groups in entirely different ways. The PSI survey of Londoners (carried out in 1981) showed that for all adults the proportion of their contacts with the police that were adversarial was 14 per cent; but this rose to 19 per cent for white men, 35 per cent for white men aged 15 to 24, 48 per cent for West Indian men and 63 per cent for West Indian men aged 15 to 24 (Smith, 1983). As to differences according to sex and age, the findings from the British Crime Survey are consistent with this, though the patterns are blurred since no analysis in terms of numbers of contacts has been published (see Southgate and Ekblom, 1984). These findings show that, while the contacts that most people have with the police are mostly amiable, there are wide differences between population groups in the nature of their police encounters, and there are some small groups whose contacts with the police are mostly adversarial. The PSI survey also shows stark contrasts in views about the police (especially about police misconduct) between different age and ethnic groups; and an intensive analysis shows that the difference in the mix of experience is the most important reason for the difference in views. Where policing is concerned, there is not one public, but many publics (Whittaker, 1979).

It is not at all surprising that this should be so. The function of the police is to enforce the law and maintain order, by force if necessary. Therefore, policing is about dealing with conflict, and even if force is not often used, the fact that it is legitimately available is the fundamental determinant of the nature of police work (the clearest expression of this point is by Egon Bittner (1975) in his book about the function of policing). To the extent that society is stratified, or at any rate differentiated, it is inevitable that law enforcement and order maintenance will impinge on some groups more than others (will be at the expense of some groups and for the benefit of others). Research does, of course, show that a belief in the need for law enforcement and order maintenance - in the need for a police force - is very general, extending even to those groups who tend to be hostile to the police. But although young West Indians are not nihilist or anarchist, their perspective on policing is very different indeed from that of white old-age pensioners.

The idea of community does not seem to provide us with a model for dealing with these conflicts. It is an idea that is best adapted to mobilising the support of the respectable majority for tough law enforcement and order maintenance. This may be useful for a time, but the problem for the police is that they have to live with the groups who bear the brunt of law enforcement and order maintenance. The idea of community cannot be successfully applied to policing if it is used to avoid finding the forms and institutions needed to strike a balance between conflicting demands.

Decentralisation versus the framework of law

Policing unfolds within the framework of the law, taking that to include the law in action as well as the law in the books. It is in the nature of the law to be impersonal, universal and, as far as possible, consistent. This appears to be in conflict with the idea that policing should be decentralised and respond to the demands of local communities. Indeed, at the extreme, law enforcement and order maintenance that is a response to the demands of local communities is equivalent to the rule of the lynch mob. The whole purpose of the law, it may be said, is to help us escape from the arbitrary judgements of our neighbours. There are surely exceptional difficulties, therefore, in applying the idea of community to an institution that is intimately related to the law.

The argument that has just been put draws attention to an important problem that must be addressed by proponents of community policing. There is a way of dealing with the difficulty: but it involves developing a framework of concepts and institutions in which the domains of universal law and local practice may be defined and coherently related to each other. Proponents of community policing have not paid much attention to this. Consequently, we have not been given a reason why community policing should not mean that nobody gets arrested for possession of drugs in the St Paul's area of Bristol (assuming that that is what the community in St Paul's wants).

A proper discussion of this issue would have to be lengthy. But it would start from the point that the pattern of policing is not *determined by* the law: rather, it forms within a broad set of constraints defined by the law. The police have a statutory duty to enforce the law, but except in rare circumstances this does not mean that the law specifies what the pattern of policing should be. Because resources are limited, the police cannot take action about all offences that come to notice, nor can they take action to discover offences of every kind: so the pattern of policing must flow from an implicit or explicit set of priorities. Also, the police may often have a choice of methods for achieving a given objective, some more abrasive than others. The messages of decentralisation, implicit in the idea of community, is that the fact of discretion, the need to make choices, should be fully recognised, and that the choices should be made at least partly in response to the wishes of local communities.

For this to be made to work, we must be able to define something called policing policy, and we must begin to be clearer about its legitimate scope, and the lines along which its territory is limited by that of English law. Also, there have to be institutions (neither the police authorities nor the consultative groups can do it at present) in which policing policy is the proper subject for discussion and negotiation between the police and local representatives.

Formal and informal controls do not fit together easily

One of the general objectives of community policies is to encourage public bodies to strengthen voluntary and informal structures and to work with rather than against them. It is interesting that commentators at all points on the political spectrum seem to assume that this can be done and differ only about how far it is desirable to do it. Proponents of community policing see formal and informal structures tenderly intertwined, like the hands of a loving mother and child. For those on the radical left, however, the mesh is like that between the rows of teeth in the upper and lower jaws of a crocodile. The idea that there is a snug fit sounds good in the abstract, but when you consider the details it is fairly hard to see how the energy in the informal structures can be tapped.

Of course it is true that order and discipline are for the most part maintained through informal social controls, or through formal controls administered by a wide range of institutions (like employers, schools and banks). In that sense it is, of course, true that the maintenance of order is the responsibility of the community as a whole: anyway, whether or not it is the community as a whole's reponsibility, the community as a whole does it.

A formal decision was taken recently to extend non-smoking regulations to all carriages on the London underground, and also to all areas beyond the ticket barriers. The result is a striking demonstration of the effectiveness of informal social controls. There have been hardly any prosecutions, and there is on the underground a very rare presence of police or staff (who seldom in any case perform a regulatory function of any kind). Nonetheless, from early morning up to about 10 pm it is rare to see anyone smoking. On late-night trains, especially on Fridays and Saturday, smoking is fairly common, but a passenger who wants to smoke will normally look into the eyes of any nearby passenger and then proceed to light up if no disapproval is shown. Thus, informal controls are effective, but they make an exception for people returning home late from parties and entertainments.

This example shows that the informal controls are enormously important, and that they are intimately related to the formal rules: before the change in the regulations, informal controls did not, of course, prevent smoking in smoking carriages, which were in fact thick with fumes and had a layer of cigarette ends on the floor. The informal controls have worked so as to implement the new rule, but with a degree of flexibility.

In the case of controlling smoking on the underground, this seems very satisfactory. Neither the police nor any police-like agency had any part in what happened. All the authorities did was to change the formal rule and put up non-smoking stickers. The informal controls did the rest. On the face of it, therefore, there is no problem about stopping people from smoking cannabis or using cocaine or heroin. All you have to do is mobilise the informal social controls. Unfortunately, however, sticking up 'no cannabis' signs in the Black and White Club in the St Paul's area of Bristol would not be followed by the mobilisation of enormously effective informal controls on the use of ganja; and 'no shooting up' signs in the men's lavatories at Piccadilly Circus would be similarly ineffective. In these instances, the informal controls and the formal regulations would just not fit.

Although the subject is important, this is not the place to pursue it further. The point that has been established is that just emphasising the importance of informal controls in a general way (or of formal controls by private bodies) does not take us very far. Most of the difficult problems for law enforcement and order maintenance arise when informal controls are *not* working to produce the desired result. The problem - and perhaps the blessing - is that informal controls cannot readily be controlled - or manipulated - by public policy. If proponents of community policies think they can be, they need to say exactly how.

Policing, crime prevention and the distribution of resources

It is generally accepted that community activity can in itself do nothing about poverty. Yet there are very important links between poverty and crime and disorder. Crime rates vary radically between areas, and all high crime areas are areas of low incomes, high unemployment and relatively high levels of social disadvantages of various kinds. At the same time, there is no simple, one-to-one relationship between crime and disorder on the one hand and social and economic deprivation of the other. Most poor people are not criminals and crime is much higher on some council estates in depressed areas than on others. Nevertheless, there is an important relationship of some kind.

So far, success has not often been demonstrated for crime prevention programmes (whether implemented by the police or by a group of agencies working together). But we have to persevere with crime prevention because no better option is available. Our knowledge is limited, but from what we do know, two things can be said with some confidence. First, successful crime prevention is likely to involve changes to the physical environment combined with community activity of various kinds. Second, crime prevention activity needs to be heavily concentrated in certain areas where the level of crime and disorder is exceptionally high. Changing the physical environment requires expenditure of funds, perhaps on a substantial scale. There also has to be expenditure on the teams that are to administer crime prevention programmes.

What may be critical, therefore, is that crime prevention programmes should be adequately funded (this fits with the view that community activity will not work on its own) and that the resources should be concentrated in the areas where they are most needed. The unequal distribution of resources is all the more important in that it is easiest to mobilise community activity in fragrant suburbs and hardest in the council estates where crime prevention is most urgently needed. Indeed, the high level of crime can be seen as a symptom of the social dislocation that will make mobilisation of the community particularly hard. The difficulty here is that the idea of community does not help in the distribution of resources. As a concrete illustration of this, it becomes more difficult rather than easier for the police to distribute their resources unequally between sub-divisions if each sub-divisional commander has to justify the distribution to a local consultative group.

Conclusions

The idea of community can be a useful stimulus to thinking about policing and crime prevention provided that it is used to raise important questions rather than to duck them. Certainly the effectiveness of policing and crime prevention turns, to a considerable extent, on the links between communities and police forces. But those who are interested in these links need to consider specific questions much more closely than proponents of community policing generally have done. The following questions have been identified in this paper.

- How can the police plan their work so as to emphasise consensus-building as far as possible? What job description can we write for community police officers, and what concrete, specific tasks would it include? In future, could community police officers be the pivot of properly resourced crime prevention programmes that are effectively linked with voluntary and informal community networks?
- What institutions can be proposed to resolve the conflicting demands on the police by different communities?
- How can policing policy, within the boundaries set by the law, be defined, and how can an institutional framework be created in which it can be intelligently discussed and negotiated between the police and the various communities?
- Informal social controls are enormously powerful, and so are the controls exerted by private organisations. How can they be mobilised for crime prevention and order maintenance, and if they can be mobilised, what safeguards are needed to ensure that they are not oppressively used?
- How can we get over the problem that crime prevention is most urgently needed in the areas where social networks are weakest? How can the need to allocate crime prevention and policing resources unequally between areas be reconciled with the need for resource allocation to be the subject of discussion with the communities concerned?

References

Bittner, E. (1975) *The Function of Police in Modern Society*, New York, Jason Aronson.

Brown, D. and Iles, S. (1985) *Community Constables: a study of a policing initiative*, Research and Planning Unit Paper 30, London, Home Office.

Gordon, P. (1984) 'Community policing: towards the local police state', *Critical Social Policy*, 10.

Hope, T. (1985) *Implementing Crime Prevention Measures*, Home Office Research and Planning Unit, Research Study 86, London, HMSO.

Kelling, G., Wycroft, M.A. and Pate, T. (1980) 'Policing: a research agenda for national policy making' in R.V.G. Clarke and J.M. Hough (editors) *The Effectiveness of Policing*, Farnborough, Gower.

Morgan, J. (editor) (1984) *Community Policing*, AIC Seminar Proceedings No 4, Canberra, Australian Institute of Criminology.

Police Foundation (1981) *The Newark Foot Patrol Experiment*, Washington DC, Police Foundation.

Reiss, A. (1971) *The Police and the Public*, New Haven, York University Press.

Smith, D.J., (1983) *Police and People in London: I. a survey of Londoners*, Research Report 618, London, Policy Studies Institute.

Southgate, P. and Ekblom, P. (1984) *Contacts Between Police and Public*, Home Office Research and Planning Unit, 77, London, HMSO.

Unit, 77, London, HMSO.

Weatheritt, M. (1985) *Innovations in Policing*, London, Croom Helm.

Whittaker, B. (1979) *The Police in Society*, London, Eyre Methuen.

Willmott, P. (1984) *Community in Social Policy*, Discussion Paper 9, London, Policy Studies Institute.